# Global

## A TRAVELER'S TALES

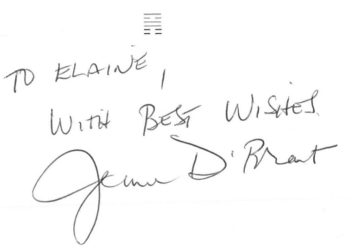

*TO ELAINE,*
*WITH BEST WISHES*
*Jeanne D'Brant*

JEANNE D'BRANT

ISBN: 978-1-7379770-0-1

Dedicated to Tony, Bob, Kevin and Malcolm

and the peoples of Afghanistan

Know the universe itself as a road, as many roads, as roads for traveling souls

Walt Whitman, Song of the Open Road

# Acknowledgments

In the current climate of polarity, intolerance, and cultural misunderstanding, it is my hope that a voice from a wider perspective will educate and hopefully enlighten the reader. Students of history and women's studies can find value in these tales recounted from a sandals-on-the-ground perspective.

I want to thank my beloved brother, William Tydeman, PhD. who always supported and believed in my writing. Because of Bill, I developed a fascination for anthropology, spending a winter immersed in his extensive collection from his days at Columbia University. That immersion was the spark for this historic journey. A heartfelt homage to Margaret Mead, PhD., for her inspiration and example. I also would like to thank the Irish American Writers and Artists Association in New York, an impressive group of creative talents, for their enthusiastic reception of my readings from this manuscript.

These stories needed to be told. The first version of the book made the rounds of publishers, led by agents with recognizable names. There was consideration for a movie. Next was the university publishing route, and strong possibilities, but through a combination of circumstances, nothing materialized. Then Afghanistan, my Afghanistan, resurged in heartbreaking scenes of evacuation and Taliban takeover, and I knew it was time to publish.

It is very different now, of course. The U.S. fought its twenty-year war, engaged believers in the dream of democracy throughout four presidencies, and then shut the door. The overland trail through the Mideast is inaccessible, its structures demolished. Pristine Ghana with its riverbanks of red sandstone has roads inland, Nigeria has had some time to grow a national identity. The skies are no longer friendly, détente was a happy ideal of ephemeral nature, peace did not come to the Middle East. The open road that once existed is now lost to history.

Other adventures await. Onward.

*Jeanne D'Brant*

*Fort Salonga, NY September 1, 2021*

# FOREWORD

I am a forensic psychologist with over 40 years' experience in the field. I have enjoyed a personal relationship with Dr. D'Brant for over 20 years and have eagerly read all drafts of the manuscript. I believe the message of the book is important for the reader who is interested in women's history and multi-cultural perspectives. I hope that Dr. D' Brant's penetrating and compassionate yet entertaining writing will lead the reader to increased tolerance and greater understanding of the issues that Afghan immigrants face in these challenging times. It is also a classic coming of age saga that chronicles the personal development of a young American woman who has the courage to explore the unknown. It's a unique voice describing a unique time and places now lost to history when Americans were welcomed and appreciated in the Middle East.

Dr. D'Brant boasts an impressive array of eclectic credentials--a degree in psychology and anthropology; decades as a Functional Medicine practitioner; a professor; author of internationally published continuing education courses as well as a published science writer, poet, and a budding a fiction writer. She brings all this knowledge and expertise to the real-life experience of extensive world-wide adventure travel and solo independent travel well outside the conventions and safe parameters of guided tours.

This is an imminently readable book that resonates with the dire current situation in Afghanistan as sharply as predicted by Dr. D'Brant's experiences there in happier times.

While the travails of our sharply rising rates of Covid-19 have rendered travel perilous for the foreseeable future, following the adventures of Jeanne D'Brant in an equally perilous time and place may provide the reader with a healthy and provocative form of entertainment.

Barbara R. Kirwin, Ph.D.

September 2021

Long Island, New York

# TABLE OF CONTENTS

**Chapter 1** The Call of the Faithful                                    1

**Chapter 2** Hairy Kisses in the  Noonday Sun                            7

**Chapter 3** Crossing the Euphrates                                     15

**Chapter 4** Helen in Persia                                            29

**Chapter 5** Dasht-i-Kavir                                              45

**Chapter 6** The Walled Citadel of Herat                                57

**Chapter 7** Rage of Purdah                                             75

**Chapter 8** Kabul                                                      87

**Chapter 9** Women's Gynecological Hospital, Kabul                      97

**Chapter 10** Death Roosts in the Khyber                               101

**Chapter 11** Passing through Pakistan                                 107

**Chapter 12** The Raj Totters On                                       115

**Chapter 13** Shahjahanpur, Uttar Pradesh                              127

**Chapter 14** Palace of Dreams                                         141

**Chapter 15** London and Coppett's Wood                                149

**Chapter 16** Flight School          159

**Chapter 17** The Hajj: Gone in Ghana      171

**Chapter 18** Sands of the Sahara       185

**Chapter 19** Hijack on the Tarmac/ Land of the Ibo     191

**Chapter 20** A Stairway in Saudi Arabia      207

**Chapter 21** Exit Africa, In Darkness      213

**Chapter 22** Peace Comes to the Middle East     219

Chapter

# 1

# THE CALL OF THE FAITHFUL

The uniformed soldier raised his gun in our direction, bayonet fixed. He had us firmly in his telescopic sights. His body pivoted as we walked, so that the rifle was always pointed squarely in our direction. Gazing at him, I saw him make an adjustment to aim the rifle directly at my head. I looked away, quickly. When we came abreast of one soldier, the next would already have us lined up in his sights. Armed men with fixed bayonets were displayed in formation along the entire span of the Meric bridge. Thus was our approach relayed at gunpoint across the bridge over the river to Edirne.

This was the only way to enter Turkey overland from Greece. A war was on, the two nations locked in bitter conflict over the issues of Cyprus and control of the Aegean. It was an old battle, reminiscent of ancient Troy and its wars with the Greek city states. Soldiers had swarmed into the northern Greek city of Thessalonika, thousands strong. The military presence continued in force across the northeast arm of the Grecian mainland along the approach to Bulgaria and Turkey.

The tales of Istanbul were of the intimidating combination of crowds, clamoring street hustlers, and chaos. I was concerned with the conditions that would greet me, fair of hair and skin, immediately obvious in the Middle East as a kaffir, an infidel. I had no Turkish or Arabic other than the few phrases I had encountered, which been used by explorers in the past. *Allah hu Akbar! God is Great! Annah dheef Allah! I am a guest of God!!* I kept the words in my journal, along with some hidden gold. White slavers were largely based in Marseilles then, but I knew a young nubile woman would fetch a fine price in these lands.

It was to be a grand adventure, traveling the ancient Silk Road through the Middle East along the corridor through Turkey, Kurdistan, Iran, Afghanistan and Pakistan to India. In my mind, the goal was total immersion in local cultures, as a neutral observer and recorder of their vanishing ways of life. A PhD. barely begun, I had surrendered the security and stifling oppression of academia for lust. Anthropologists like to call the firsthand experience of other cultures "going into the field," and the need for it was pounding a drumbeat in my veins. I had studied polygamous societies and

2

marriage rituals and initiation rites. I had sat at the feet of the great Margaret Mead, studied Bateson and Malinowski and other heavyweights of cultural anthropology and social psychology. I wanted to hear firsthand the call of the faithful, muezzins in minarets. Before globalization, there was a great sense of urgency regarding the decline of world cultures due to the all-pervasive influence of the west. An imperative had been issued to go forth, to witness and record societies before their ways of life were corrupted and lost. My goal was to journey to a people and place where a westerner had never been seen. That goal would be accomplished, albeit briefly, but now I had just begun. I would be a stranger in a strange land, but other than Iran and the western part of Turkey, most nations along the overland route through the Middle East and Afghanistan to India were not westernized, not craving our material goods, and not remotely concerned about our politics. Little attention would be paid to an American, and I suspected that to most people outside of the major cities, all non-Muslims would indistinguishable. I was an infidel, not a follower of Islam, and therefore not significant to their way of life.

Being an American guaranteed the impressive might of the American Embassy at my back. Before the taking of hostages in Teheran during the Carter era, the embassies of the Middle East were places of refuge, order, and civility. Should any difficulties arise with foreign authorities, they could be authoritatively negotiated and resolved. I remembered my third-grade teacher, Mrs.

Bruckler, sending an inattentive eight-year-old to the world map, in front of the entire class, to point out the location of Afghanistan. School maps then still featured the United States squarely in the middle of the world, with Asia's land mass neatly divided in two on either side of North America. Most Americans thought the U.S. was the proud hub of the world and were still carrying Teddy Roosevelt's big stick. We arrogantly taught our children that no other country could compare to the U.S. in power, military might, resources, affluence and prosperity. And Americans were entitled to respect as representatives of this exalted democracy anywhere in the world that they chose to travel! Other countries should be grateful to get our American dollars! After all, those other people "didn't even speak English!" Such were the prevailing attitudes of the era. The opportunities and rights of a United States citizen were supposed to be the gold standard to which all other nations aspired. A stranger in a strange land I would be, but the semi-divine right of American invincibility even had the backs of its flower children.

Because of war, my friends and I could not get a bus to the Greek/Turkish border. We were advised to find transport out of Kavala in Greece to a town about four miles away from the borders station, and to hike in. The soldiers at the bus station were clearly disturbed by our choice of destination. They shook their heads and muttered in Greek among themselves. It was hardly politically correct to mention that we were off for

Istanbul, therefore we named the last Greek town before the border and fooled no one.

I had some trepidation about the situation, although the drumbeat of road lust was just as loud in Greece as it had been in New York. This was not four-star land package. It was an independent-coming-of-age anthropological journey, unsupported by the infrastructure or financial backing of a university. In reality, it was just me, going off alone to meet the unknown. Fortune had smiled, however, by connecting me to a young American male heading to India and putting us in the path of a group of New Zealanders and Australians homeward bound across Asia. They would willingly accompany me through the upcoming rigors of the physical and emotional terrain. It was never about comfort or familiarity, it was about the chance to see how others lived and believed, and to experience their realities through them. If those observations took me one day back to grad school, so be it. Local transportation, rough buses and trucks, were to be the mode of transportation. The heat and dust and crowds only added to the authenticity.

Arabic is written in a flowing script, from right to left, with its own characters. I couldn't speak the language, or even read it. There would be no alphabet, and no numerals to recognize. How to buy food and use money that was unreadable? How to make change and not get cheated? How great was the risk for a western woman?

Stepping carefully around mosques and holy cities was imperative, a non-Muslim's presence was a considered a defilement. Respect was imperative. Then there were the fierce tribesmen, the Pushtunwali of Afghanistan, who acknowledged no outside authority or law. I knew that overland travel across the Muslim lands would be harsh, the treatment of women disturbing, the climate rigorous. The style of living would be vastly different from North America or Europe.

It was time to take the monster of the Middle East by the tail and chart a course across the unknown. In my perception, I was an American grad student anthropologist on a mission to document vanishing cultures and ways of life. In reality, I was heading across the deserts of the Middle East on public transportation with people I barely knew; I was young, blonde, and female, and surrounded by warring armies of weaponed men.

I was thrilled.

Chapter

# 2

# HAIRY KISSES IN THE
# NOONDAY SUN

The soldiers on the streets of Alexandropoulos in 1975 cavorted in the noonday sun, exchanging blossoms and kisses. Big, burly military men strolled hand in hand, playing kissy face. Their homosexuality was obvious and celebrated. None of the locals were fazed. Gay culture was still in the closet in the U.S. and the closet door was still shut. The sight of an entire army of uniformed military men openly flirting and frolicking was flabbergasting. In the Middle East, a properly modest woman never looks a man in the eye. I could hardly look away from these guys! My companions were jittery, unexpectedly confronting whole new parameters of acceptable male behavior. They made jokes, but it was these straight Western men who walked on the streets with their eyes downcast and their faces averted. I came to find the whole situation very humorous. We were witnessing a celebration of the sweetness of being lovers in the bright sunshine of the day, and none of my dumbfounded traveling group, whether from London or Philadelphia or Adelaide or Perth, had ever seen the like of it before.

The Turkish soldiers looked little different from the Greek, to my unschooled eye. I sought details of attitude, expression, bearing, but the masses in uniform overwhelmed my powers of discrimination. It was not acceptable to watch particular men at length, or to gauge their social interactions in a studied fashion, and admitting to myself that they all looked alike, at least in uniform, revealed a disturbing lack of observational skills. The women had begun to look far more Old World as we headed east, ever closer to the Asian continent. Short, stocky, and kerchiefed, they were dressed completely in black down to their sturdy shoes and thick woolen stockings. As the sight of these women became more common, hot showers and flush toilets were already a thing of the past. The Greek sun beat down on the dusty roads and pine trees. Western civilization was slipping away.

Climbing off yet another bus onto a dry and dusty plain, we began the trek into Turkey. After a few miles of walking in the hot sun, the Meric River appeared. It was a lovely day when we crossed the bridge at the border. A fresh breeze had sprung up, smelling of hot pine and baked stones. The river tossed and sparkled in the wind, reflecting blue skies. I trotted across that bridge to the beginning of the Muslim lands with a lilt in my step that no soldiers with fixed bayonets could diminish. We did not acknowledge them, and in our minds, we had lessened their power.

Crossing into Turkey, the pace and noise level became exponential. General motion was towards Istanbul, teeming crowds and cabs and trucks and buses. I stood, parched and flat-footed in the dust, until a truck taxi with an Israeli woman inside pulled up. Piling in, it was all aboard for the ancient city formerly known as Constantinople. I drew confidence from the presence of that woman, a Jew with gonads enough to be in a Muslim country alone. Raven-haired and green eyed, she was the first Israeli that I had ever met. Off of her kibbutz for a summer of travel in the Mideast, her passport, emblazoned with the Star of David, created not a ripple.

Historically, Istanbul had been Constantinople, and in its earlier incarnation, Byzantium. As the gateway to the Holy land, control of Constantinople had been the goal of the Crusaders. It was largely the lies of Alexius I, its Christian emperor, which had incited the First Crusade. Concerned about threats to his control of major trade routes, Alexius asked the pope for a contingent of knights, the armored tanks of the era. Urban II had his own motives for supporting the request. The claims of Alexius that Christian monks were being raped by Muslim warriors had a huge impact on medieval Europe. An outraged Urban II called for a holy war to defend Christendom. A Christian Jihad was on! Peter the Hermit, a mild-mannered vegetarian cleric, rose up in horror, calling for the peasants to help rid the Holy Land of the Muslim scourge and, incidentally, strengthen Urban's power in the east. The Peasants' Crusade, twenty thousand strong, pillaged and raped south and east across Europe. While Muslims were few and far between, Jews were not. Five thousand Jews perished in this forgotten Holocaust, buried in mass graves in the Rhineland. Alexius got the avenging peasant horde across the Bosporus, where they fell on the Turkish Christian city of Nicaea. They couldn't tell the locals apart either. They killed every Christian in sight. The Seljuk Turks then annihilated the Crusaders to a man. Thus ended the Peasants' Army, but the Crusades had just begun.

The ancient port city now called Istanbul straddled two continents. Europe ends at the Bosporus, where Asia begins. The Haga Sophia and the Topkapi Palace still stood, monuments to the ages for fifteen centuries. There were no traffic lights in Istanbul then, but every checkered cab on the planet was there. The place was a cacophony of honking horns and squealing tires. The smell of burning brake linings polluted the air, and the roads were without rules. Road rage was old news in the Mideast long before it happened in L.A.

As the truck slowed, we were set upon by a screeching mob of men, dressed in a mix of robes and western clothing. Climbing out reluctantly, we were walled off by the human traffic and separated into twos or threes. A dozen or more beseeching men tried pushing us forcibly into cars.

Hands tried to yank away our luggage, the better to coerce us to follow the grabber and thereby mark us as his. Once this type of commitment was made to a particular "guide," the others turned away to find new prey. These men received a commission from the hotel that they fronted for, from the cab company that did the transportation, from the vendors in the bazaar who were recommended by the hotel, and so on up the food chain. Every society has its dregs, these men were bottom feeders.

I had a hotel picked out before we got there, a place for budget travelers and internationals to rest, gather information and exchange news of the road. The BIT information guide out of London, the equivalent Fodor's guide for overland travelers, listed several recommendations for this particular hotel. I went in expecting a rustic version of a pensione to find something else entirely. Dried blood was splashed on the walls. The room hadn't seen a mop since the Crusades. Old cots without linens served as the beds. There was a squatter down the hall, smeared with blood and feces, a dirty shower and a filthy sink. It was so unbearably hot and rank, I didn't think I could ever sleep. So, this was Istanbul. Budget Istanbul, at least, for the backpacking, grad student, adventurer set. The stories had been too right. I didn't admit to wanting a clean bed in a comfortable room. This was the field, I knew that. Hardships were part of the adventure. I was tough enough. Wasn't I?

Thousands of land miles lay ahead, now framed in dark imaginings. Had I made the right choice, trying to do this independently, without the backing or safety net of a major university? This trip was supposed to be the ultimate freelance adventure. I would go where the wind blew me and watch the moon wax and wane in desert skies. Following my instincts, I would be a witness to the untouched and the unknown. I was leaving the war machine superpower for a journey through time, to less developed, iconic, and teeming places. Hot, exotic places with strange smells and hypnotic gazes above veiled faces. Would it always be this difficult?

My new friend from New Zealand, Tony, came to my rescue that first oven-like night in Asia. Tony was a half-Scottish, half Japanese North Islander. He invited me to the roof of the hotel, where a congenial gathering was transpiring. The full moon shone over the Bosporus, which glinted darkly in the distance. A breeze, aromatic with spice, stirred the air. At last, at last, a respite from the chaos. I lay gratefully on my sleeping bag on the cooling concrete of the roof, watching the breeze ruffle distant shadows of palm fronds. The city below was dim, quiet, lit mostly by oil lamps. Suddenly, the call to prayer boomed out, muezzins in the minarets. It was the personification of the voice of the unknown; foreign, harsh, unbearably exotic. Chills ran down my spine.

Visas for Iran would take a few days, leaving time to explore the city. There were markets and museums, Topkapi Palace, and the Blue Mosque. Non-Muslims were tolerated at this mosque, although I saw few women. It was an exquisite place; blue and white, full of space and light and prostrate men in robes and headdresses. Each tile was a treasure of loving detail. Like the cathedrals built on ancient Druid sites in Europe, and the basement chapels of the Vatican in Rome, there was a strong sense of presence in that place.

No visit to Istanbul would have been complete without a visit to Yenner's. Yehudi Yenner's restaurant was a hangout for the local international set. It was said that Yenner would never refuse anyone a meal, whether or not they had the money to pay for it. Perhaps it was healthy profits made in the illicit drug trade. More likely, it was the famous Islamic hospitality, mandated in the Qur'an. Yenner's was the Studio 54 of the era, the hippest and most happening spot in town.

Walking one day in the slanted sunlight of a late afternoon, I saw a Dutch couple whom I had first met in Belgium. Determined to be respectful of the local modes of dress and to attract as little attention as possible, I traveled with several escorts. Modesty required the wearing of a long-sleeved shirt over my long skirt and tank top, and I also had donned a small head scarf. The Dutch woman, a nurse, had disdained wearing a tunic or long skirt, and walked the streets of Istanbul hand in hand with her man, publicly displaying affection. She was bareheaded, dressed only in flowery capri pants and a tank top. Her gluteii were maximus, ample buttocks jouncing with her every step. Turkish men were lined up on both sides of her path, frenzied. They tore at their faces and hair in delirious admiration of her jiggling rump. One fellow, transported in delight by the sight of this forbidden munificence walking nonchalantly down the street, tore off his head gear and stomped it into the sidewalk as the other men cheered. This display, in the relative urbanity of Istanbul, convinced me to pay very close attention to local mores. When in Byzantium, do as the Byzantines do, and watch your ass.

Chapter

# 3

# CROSSING THE EUPHRATES

The veiled woman by the river bent to fill her water jar. She was middle-aged, in her late twenties, and dressed completely in black. Her heavy head scarf was wrapped about her neck and shoulders, as befit a modest woman, but her white veil was unclasped at the side of her face. Catching sight of me, she stood as if rooted, her dark-eyed gaze transfixed. Silhouetted against the sun, her body rigid, she emanated shock.

A tall woman dressed in blue climbed wearily off a bus by the edge of a river. Her pale skin was flushed pink in the heat. Her neck was bare, as were her ankles and sandaled feet. She wore no veil, just a strange garment over her skirt, decorated with embroidery. Yellow hair hung down her back. Where was her husband? She walked alone, head up, alert for danger. When she took off her dark glasses, her eyes were blue green. Was she a jinn?

The women shared little other than their gender. One was a daughter of the desert, raised in the blistering heat of the burning stones and dust. Her people veiled their women and hid them behind walls, the property of men, with no civil rights. The other was thousands of miles from home, traveling alone, risking life and limb for adventure and learning and answers to questions she could not yet ask. The dark daughter had little education, and all she had seen of the world lay between her nearby mud brick home and this water source on the Euphrates. She had never known electricity; no television or news of the outside world penetrated the confines of her existence. She cooked over a fire or in a brick oven, her days spent in the arduous tasks of preparing her family's meals. It was likely that she had married at fourteen.

The yellow-haired woman had married once and found him not to her liking. She had her own car and telephones and favorite restaurants. She read books and took ballet lessons and drew in charcoals and went to therapy. In her world, family was fragmented and distant. Wealth and competition were the gods, the acquisition of goods was supposed to bring happiness. She was the product of a culture that had lost touch with the rhythms of the natural world.

The desert daughter had her place in her large family. Her role was fixed and often subservient. She owned almost nothing but a few clothes and her jewelry. She had a home, and a place, a future, and a family to live with for life. Her existence was ordered by the climate and the changing seasons, and by her religion, which defined all things and her proper response to them.

They stared at each other across the chasm of their diversity in utter fascination. One rested with her sister-wives and in-laws in the shade of the trees by her Euphrates home. The other sat as an equal with five men who offered cool drinks and conversation for her pleasure. They never spoke a single word to each other, just drank in each other's world with their eyes, each allowing the other's unending observation in exchange for being allowed her own.

It was then that I realized that I had attained the holy grail. She had never seen the infidel before. I was a kaffir, her first. I had realized the anthropologist's dream.

Back on the bus, the cooling shade of trees and river were all too soon lost, as the cross-country journey recommenced. For three days out of Istanbul, we bounced along an often unpaved and dusty road riddled with giant potholes. My arms were green with bruises, the road strewn with metallic corpses. Parts were impossible to get out here, when a rig broke down, it was abandoned, roadkill. I was relieved to be out of Istanbul, where the traffic had left one in serious peril for one's life. Crossing over the Bosporus had had a sense of finality. I kept turning around to gaze at the last of Europe, knowing that this journey would indelibly alter who I was. I had breached the end of the western world, and in so doing, contracted with the unknown. Whatever came my way, I had agreed to step off that edge. On the wide, dark plains of Anatolia, my decision had far more weight than it did on the sunlit beaches of Greece.

The bus pushed east for days and nights without pause, except for infrequent stops for the driver to nap and eat. We called him Bruno, for his size and huge ham-like fists. Bruno was affable and kind. He wore western clothing and a wide smile, and was surrounded by his "cousins," who served as lookouts and go-fers. They were palpably proud of their association with the man driving the big rig. The youth and excitement of some of them were endearing. We spoke no Turkish but Bruno had some French. He did not know New York, although London got a nod of recognition.

One of Bruno's hangers-on was different. An older, skinny, slimy man, he wore too-short polyester pants, had a rat's face, and a bad odor. From the way he looked at me, I knew there would be trouble.

My guard was up, but so were my feminist principles. I was young, self- righteous, outraged at the condescension and treatment of females. I would not bow my head and avert my eyes for the sake of this stinking bastard. His stares became more insolent, and he developed a habit of brushing against me when he paced the aisle of the bus, his trespasses increasing insidiously.

It pained me not to be able to handle the situation on my own, but I realized that he carried a knife, and in his world what he would understand best was another man staking his claim. So, I asked Malcolm Armstrong to be my "husband" for this part of the journey.

I had five male companions, and my blood sang for two of them. The choice was between Malcolm and Kevin, a rugged Australian vs. an artistic New Zealander. Malc was pleased to be chosen, he moved to the aisle seat, and we decided to exchange our rings for show. I soon came to learn that a ring on the third finger, left hand had absolutely no meaning out here. There were other conflicts too. It was going to be a long trip, in close quarters with five men. They were my protection posse, sent to me by the gods and goddesses divine on the Greek Isles. I must admit, I was enjoying being the American beauty on the road. I had a strong connection with both of these men. Kevin was beautiful and sensitive, blue eyed and long haired, with the Celtic soul of the artist he was. I thought I would fall in love if I went there, and that was too much of a complication for my plans. Malcolm was blond and righteous, a pragmatic Australian with a keen intelligence. If I had to play the role of damsel in distress, I thought Malc better suited to the sword and shield.

Bruno liked me too. He would look in the rear-view mirror and boom out "Madame, you my? Monsieur no good." This would send everyone rolling with laughter. "MAAHHHDAM, you my?" became a constant repetition, heard every five minutes, road hour after road hour, the din of male laughter crashing in my ears. I was shaken and miserable, in truth, the intensity of Istanbul had overwhelmed me. Din, dirt, naked aggression, intolerance, all had left me feeling assaulted. The men were demented, following me everywhere, peering through peepholes in the walls of the shower, accosting me in the hallways of the hotel.

I had no privacy, no respite, now Bruno and his Slimy friend hounded me during the endless ride, and my slightest foray off of the bus brought immediate, relentless attention. There were no toilets, I had to learn to urinate standing up with my legs spread wide. I couldn't turn my back and pull a hose out of my clothes, I couldn't wear panties, and the lack of underwear only enhanced the feeling of vulnerability.

Istanbul is on as isthmus surrounded by the Black Sea to the north and the Sea of Marmara to the south. As such, it was considerably cooler than the desert that we were now crossing. I wondered morosely how anyone could tolerate such a climate. Slimy seemed to take pity on my wilted state and unfurled a sleeping bag across the back seat of the bus. His hand motions suggested repeatedly and convincingly that I should lie down in the back and take some rest. Could I really have been that much of an innocent? A space to lie flat had much appeal after days of sleeping in a sitting position. The lack of food, the heat-induced daze and the rhythm of the wheels soon brought about a state of semi-consciousness. I vaguely felt the bus slow down as we pulled into a little roadside chaikana. Too tired to get up, I dozed.

The hands under my skirt woke me with a start. I pushed them away frantically, trying to sit up. Slimy jumped me, grabbing everywhere, pulling. I smacked his face and fought for all I was worth. He kept trying to push me down, and with hammering heart I struck back. We fell off the seat onto the floor, rolling, he trying to get my skirt up, me fighting in a defensive panicked adrenalin rush. It was a terrible thrashing interval, and any rational thoughts of appropriately placed kicks or kneeing him in the balls never entered my mind. I just kept hitting him, fending off his attempts to wrestle me down and get my skirt up. Eventually, I came to realize that his attempts were weakening. Perhaps he had not expected resistance. He finally moved away from me and I stood, panting, fixing my clothes. He was still between me and the door, I would have to get all the way to the front of the bus to get to safety. Slimy walked to the door with his shoulders slumped, head down, the very picture of dejection. As I passed him to descend the bus stairs, he stuck out his hand to shake. A Muslim woman would never have shaken his hand, nor would he have offered. But I was American, and naïve; the gesture, I thought, was in part an acknowledgement of his cultural misunderstanding. He seemed to have thought I would be willing. I observed the body language of defeat, his bent head and stooped posture, and saw the proffered hand. I hesitated, deciding, and then magnanimously shook. Immediately his other hand swooped up, grabbed a handful of breast, and squeezed, leering his triumph. Furious, humiliated, and endangered again by my own innocence, I fled.

Malcolm and the others tried to redeem their failure of my defense at leaving me sleeping on the bus by scowling at Slimy at every opportunity. Getting into it, they began bumping and tripping him for sport. He gathered his homeboys around him, eyeing us. It was bad vibes all around. We were six foreigners on a bus ride that could easily be our last. The American Embassy would never find out what happened to me, out here no one had even heard of the USA! These men were on home turf, city-dwellers raised on robbery. We were all afraid of being knifed. I no longer found any humor in "Madame, you my?" The ride went on forever. The diesel fuel reeked; the desert burned. The mountains were red, green, and gray, snow striped in the distance. Filth and sweat and stink filled my nostrils, some of it my own.

We had no idea of what to eat, so we ate very little. Sometimes we were taken into kitchens of the little roadside places where we stopped. Nothing was recognizable. It was probably lentils and lamb, good Middle Eastern food, but it all looked like mystery mush. We lived on pita bread and red onions. Coca Cola and Fanta were everywhere, we thought them safe until another traveler told us that they were bottled in country, with local water. The natural flora and fauna here were very foreign. Even if the water were devoid of pathogens, drinking it was still an unacceptable risk.

A smiling tribesman pointed out the window and cried "Noah's Ark"! Mount Ararat loomed in the distance. The excited bus crew stopped the vehicle and invited us to go out and explore the site where the Ark had supposedly landed. A few trusting souls climbed off the bus to investigate. No longer a trusting soul, my anthropological idealism seriously compromised by pessimism regarding human nature, I thought it might be a ruse to separate us from our luggage. I could see a return to an empty plateau after poking about the stony ruins. We would probably be told that there was no bus, never had been a bus, and just exactly what did we think we were doing there anyway?

The driver smiled on, and eventually I softened. The cast of characters had changed. These men were the real deal, not big city hustlers. They wore robes and headdresses and most carried rifles casually slung over their shoulders. They offered us food and stopped the bus when someone was sick or wanted a photo. The bus now stopped frequently, in stone villages where the men greeted each other like long-lost brothers. Banners flapped in the breeze, festooning our stops. Children played and dogs raced in the sun. Despite the presence of foreign men on the bus, a few women even appeared, smiling shyly and offering food while watching the children. I felt like we were guests at a gaily decorated festival, and although we appeared to be very strange and foreign indeed, their hospitality allowed us to be included, extended family. Welcoming faces were everywhere. I considered asking to stay.

This was Kurdistan, the large eastern majority of the country of Turkey. Kurdistan, the nation without a state, was divided by the political borders of four countries. The large Kurdish population of Iraq lay a few hours to the south. Nearby Syria and Iran also had a sizable number of Kurds. The nation had been divided since the 14th century, when spoils of war gave the northern part to the Ottoman Empire and the rest became part of Persia. Further division by the British and their allies splintered the Kurds across many national borders, with resultant severe consequences to their culture and national identity. It was illegal to speak the Kurdish language in Turkey then, but high in their mountain domain, the yoke of governmental policy stretched thin. My ear could discern that the words used among these proud warrior types became a different language in the presence of other locals. The Peshmerga ("those who face death") looked upon the Turks as the enemy. The first bus crew from Istanbul had been shunned by these friendly people of the stony plateaus.

The mountain where Noah's Ark had allegedly made landfall stood 10,000 feet above sea level.

The plateau of Kurdistan was itself at 6,000 feet, yet Mt. Ararat was still impressive in a stark way.

Earthquakes rocked the Richter scale on a frequent basis here, killing tens of thousands at a clip. Because of the altitude, the six-month winters were harsh, leaving permanent snow cover on the sharp aggressive peaks. The resources of the area were water and oil. The snows and rainfall provided arable land, the oil reserves were some of the richest in the Middle East. Oil and water, the two that never mix.

Despite the natural richness of the land, the breathtaking vistas of mountain and gorge, and the warmth of the Kurds I encountered, I felt deeply uneasy. Perhaps it was the result of the assault. Perhaps it was the first-hand experience of an admittedly myopic view of the intensity of Turkish culture, followed by planet Kurdistan. I could sense a deep and explosive tension within a country that I had assumed wore a uniform face. Even among themselves, the Kurds were known to be clannish, following their own tribal leaders, reminiscent of the Highland Scots. Tribal identity was a far more consuming issue than I had any concept of. The lands of the Middle East were not divided into neat little packages of language and culture, and assessable risk, by national borders. If I were to survive this journey, I would need to alter my thinking considerably.

Malcolm and I were tired of playing young marrieds. I was grouchy and irritable, he sneezed and snuffled. I wanted Kevin to take over the husband role. I considered the pleasant prospect for an entire afternoon, casting him lazy smiles with full eye contact. A few of the Kurds, who had been affable and always grinning, began to stiffen and talk amongst themselves.

I had slept with all the guys together in a single room whenever the luxury of beds had been available. It would have been an unfathomable risk for me to sleep in a room alone. We had stopped camping on the beach back in Kavala, when the swarming army of Greek soldiers had taken me out of the comfort zone of sleeping outside on the ground. Kevin had been hurt that I had chosen Malcolm first. Kevin's pride and letting Malc off the hook gently were much on my mind.

Bruno and Slimy long gone, our Kurdish bus crew was now hauling ass for the Irani border. I was hesitant to switch "husbands" under their very noses. The vibe had changed considerably when I began casting sultry looks at Kevin. So Malcolm and I miserably endured the heat and each other with the snapping irritability of the long wed. To his credit, he hung in there, allowing me to follow my instincts and stay by him.

Later, I learned of the Kurdish practice of "honor Killing." It sanctions the murder by a male family member of a woman who had allegedly "shamed" her family. The grounds for the killing of women are three: being a victim of rape, having an out-of-wedlock pregnancy, and the choosing of one's own husband!

I had been about to commit an offense punishable by death in this society. It was an anthropological blunder of the highest order. How would they have handled such behavior in a foreigner? I was on their turf, being put off the bus alone could have been a death sentence. Would they have expected Malcolm to do me violence had I made a move toward Kevin? Would they have done it themselves? These warm-hearted people had that capability? The men who smiled and indulged me with sweets and smiles killed women who chose a husband outside of an arranged marriage? It was chilling, unfathomable.

My lapse was also deeply disturbing. Not violating local mores was a cardinal rule for any field observer. In my emotional distress after Istanbul and the near rape, followed by the lulling warmth of Kurdish hospitality, I had forgotten the rules. There were so many ways to do harm out here, and to get oneself killed.

After leaving Mt. Ararat in the late afternoon, the bus swung northeast through the purpling Taurus Mountains towards Iran. As darkness descended, we crossed the border to the land of Reza Shah Pahlavi, the feared dictator du jour whose secret police were known to target the young and the foreign. Iran was considered to

27

be the most politically dangerous country on the overland trail, a place to lay low, stay clean and get out of Dodge fast. Next stop, Teheran.

Chapter

# 4

# HELEN IN PERSIA

M y face at the window dropped them like flies. Bedlam was in the eyes of the beholders. Males of the species, rapt, raced to jump aboard the big bus, their previous intentions forgotten. They fought each other for the privilege of lining up to negotiate my price with my traveling companions. Some spoke English, others had none. Some gave up quickly, their body language evincing defeat, others rode on for hours, confident that theirs was the bid that would be taken.

I was not unfamiliar with being the target of unwelcome attentions, or of creating chaos just by walking down the street. America before Gloria Steinem was genderist to the point of absurdity. My mother would draw disparaging "woman driver" comments simply by pulling into a gas station. Walking anywhere after the age of eleven left me vulnerable to cat calls, wolf whistles and jeers. It was "American Girl in Italy, 1951" [1] on a constant basis. Men drove right off the roads or hit dividers while gaping at me. Although I had drawn that kind of attention since early adolescence, never had my looks cast such a spell so powerfully for so many. It was overwhelming, disturbing. I feigned disinterest, heart beating rapidly in alarm, keeping a close covert watch on the situation. It did not make for a peaceable journey.

My friends Malcolm, Kevin, Bob and Tony talked for hours with those who spoke English. There were lengthy discussions on the customs of east and west, and the norms of gender roles and behaviors. Politeness was de rigueur and the subject of the terms of my availability was always addressed obliquely. My traveling companions obviously enjoyed the attention. Malcolm told me later that the persistent ones never doubted that my friends had the power to close the deal. Some left the bus angry and frustrated by my companions for holding out, a tactic of very skilled bargainers. Sensing my deep unease, Malc refused to reveal how much money they had been offered, but I saw that he was amazed and dazed by what had transpired.

How well did I know these guys? They could have made their fortunes arranging for my future in Purdah. Gold for a golden-haired woman, or at least serious baksheesh. The earnestness and the length of the negotiations were what unnerved me, although all meaningful bargaining in this part of the world was lengthy. The men lined up, each awaiting his turn, urban fellows with expensive suits and wrist watches, fine-featured, dark, and often handsome. After the initial assessment, they did not look at me, my reactions to the situation chillingly deemed irrelevant. Some of them rode the whole day.

The villages in the distance were remote, seemingly devoid of life. Mud-baked walls, rectangular roof lines; they were colorless, blending into the monochrome of the desert. Cities of Dune. (2) What could life be like behind those walls? Rarely could be glimpsed the sight of barefoot veiled women in the distance carrying water jugs on their heads, their gait a smooth glide. The trick, I later learned, is to listen to the music of the water slapping hollowly on the inside of the jug and to create, via gait, a constant rhythm. The women loped along, dark figures in the distance, long veils streaming out behind them, the music of their heavy stone jugs ordering their pace. Mostly, the vistas were of mud-baked fortresses looming out of the rock of the desert, surrounded by walls, absent of the slightest sign of life. Except for the shrines. Shrines to the ancient, pagan, pre-Islamic goddesses could be seen, stone niches holding fruit and even blossoms, standing surprising testament to continued reverence for ancient ways.

Tabriz was a shock, with its carnival atmosphere and electric lights. It had a roundabout, a circular loop of outlying road that eventually led the approaching traveler to the city within. This quintessentially British touch bespoke the connection between the ruler's modernization campaign and his western leanings. Metal archways stood at the entrance of the roundabout, festooned with strings of lights and portraits of the absolute monarch, Shah Mohammed Reza Pahlavi. The effect was quite astounding. In the midst of the burning stone desert and dirt-poor medieval villages, periodically the road took us driving in circles under clear electric Christmas lights! It seemed that these towns had little to offer the current century, beyond the unexpected zap of light.

It was a long hot ride to Teheran, and it would be even longer to Afghanistan. Besides the physical surround, there was the trepidation of the secret police, the dreaded Savak. Like Saddam Hussein, Reza Shah ruled his country with an iron fist. It was known that his secret police had infiltrated even the Irani student enclaves at foreign universities, alert for dissidents. Their methods were brutal. The Shah used his country's oil residues to purchase his favorite toys, F-14 tomcats. He bailed out the troubled aerospace industry on Long Island with a single contract which kept the F-14 program alive, the engineers employed, and the economy rolling. He was a hero at the Grumman Aerospace Corporation, where I worked summers during college. My father, a Grumman executive, knew the Shah and admired him. Pahlavi was viewed as a benevolent Big Daddy with deep pockets. Grumman had a technical support program that sent hundreds of engineers to Iran for six-month stints, helping the Iranian air force to maintain the Shah's high-tech toys. It was the height of Pahlavi's "White Revolution," his ambitious plan to modernize Iran, create land reform, and extend voting rights to women. While beloved in the west, his despotism and brutal methods seeded the ground for the revolution that made Islamic fundamentalism the dominant political force in the Middle East.

The mullahs were not ready for women's rights, and the gap between the urban upper classes and the poor peasants became a yawning chasm. The Shah brought a large foreign presence onto Iranian soil, foreigners with decadent ways who partied with a ruler already known for abuses and excessive sexual appetites. The rich got richer and emulated the unbelievers, while the barefoot poor remembered the proscription of the Qu'ran that one's Islamic nature is compromised by mimicking the unworthy ways of the infidel. The imperialist and corrupt Shah would finally be driven out of his country, cancer-ridden and friendless, to die a pariah on foreign soil.

Pre-revolutionary Teheran looked in many places like an American city. Western clothing was displayed in the shop windows, and the tony districts sported wide landscaped boulevards and Mercedes Benz. The haves and have-nots were clearly demarcated, Irani women in smart suits and Italian leather shoes shopped the equivalents of Rodeo Drive and Fifth Avenue, while poor women veiled to the eyebrows walked barefoot in the bazaars. Everywhere were billboards for Coca-Cola. Fashionable shops had Westernized mannequins in white bridal gowns on almost every corner. It was an odd fascination, this thing for American-looking brides in white. I did not know then that Paradise in Islam is depicted as a place of fair-haired virgins in long flowing dresses. The forty virgins that Mohammed Atta thought he was heading for when he gunned his hijacked airplane into the North Tower on September 11 were mostly light-skinned blondes. There is a terrible irony in that.

Persia was a long way from Paris, yet Teheran before the Islamic revolution resonated of both of LA and the City of Lights. Language, alphabet, and numbers were completely different from their European counterparts, yet the atmosphere of elegant sophistication in certain parts of town was unmistakable. Surprisingly, very little English was spoken, it was quite difficult for Westerners to find their way around. Polite formality greeted attempts to ask for directions or information, the main impediment being not unwillingness but language.

Westernization aside, this was a police state, and the Shah was under pressure from his Western allies to appear to be stopping the trafficking in drugs. His response was to crack down on the merchants and the hippies, while the big international deals went on. His police seemed to focus on the little people of Teheran, the shopkeepers and merchants, the terrified restauranteurs.

It was law that every public establishment had to have a portrait of the Shah prominently displayed, and a second one of his wife, Fara Diba, or his son, or the royal family together. Shah, Shah-ess, Shah-ing, they all sternly gazed down upon their public, huge, unsmiling, and self-important. These omnipresent three foot by four foot black and white images created a monotonous and monstrous fascist presence watching over one's every move.

Malcolm walked into a shop one afternoon and commented on the beauty of the empress. He was immediately informed that it was an insult to the Shah, or any man, to make any comment about his wife. Surprised, he began to explain Western customs to the merchant. The man then informed him that it was local belief that in the west, if a man wanted a woman, he simply walked up to her on the street and took her. He had learned this from movies, he said. Perhaps this explained some of the behavior of the would-be lotharios on the bus. No preliminaries, no consent necessary, just decide you want her and make it happen. The culture gap was a chasm.

We learned not to laugh or smile or talk too loudly anywhere on the streets of Teheran, for such behavior was suspect. The secret police were everywhere. This repressed and paralyzed society would spawn a revolution that would bring the Ayatollah Khomeini to power and give Islamic Fundamentalism legitimacy as a governing force. It would also cripple the administration of the peacemaker president, Jimmy Carter. What if the Shah had not railroaded his nation toward modernization? If he were democratic and not a despot? What if his brutal regime had embraced a return to Persian high culture and not been in bed with the West? The Twin Towers might still be standing, the screams and deaths nonexistent. Osama bin Laden, on his high horse, could have galloped towards another target. It was the relentless heavy-handedness of Pahlavi that gave the mullahs cause to consider Westernization as anti-Islamic.

Often the urban Teheranis did not know what to make of us. Westerners, obviously, but backpacked and sandaled and not on track for conspicuous consumption. Academics were suspect under the Shah's regime. It was, after all, Irani students in foreign countries who actually dared to speak out loud of their dissatisfactions with his government.

Accommodations were limited. The Amir Kabir hotel, popular among overlanders, was our destination, but we had to find it first. The sun had gone over the horizon hours before, accommodations were urgent. The interim place we finally chose looked like a rundown version of a scene from the Arabian Nights.[3] It had an indoor courtyard with palm trees, balconies overlooking the cool green oasis, and thick, worn, Persian carpets. Our passports were unequivocally demanded by the hotel desk clerk. Warnings abounded all along the trail to never give up one's passport, even briefly. Because the clerk was adamant and the hour so late, the documents were uneasily surrendered. We sat on the floor of our room, overlooking the courtyard, sipping chai and drinking in the view. A few of the guys went down to the street to score some hash. Rich, black, fragrant, ass-kicking hashish, and were those silver streaks opium? Was it worth risking the firing squad? The courtyard with its gently swaying palms and foreign cacophony became the window to another world.

Suddenly, the peaceful reverie was shattered. Tony burst into the room in total panic. Police were downstairs, asking questions. General pandemonium broke out, hiding the evidence, panicked fear of impending arrest. Was it the Savak, the Shah's dreaded force? Would we be taken off and never seen again? What would be the fate of the foolish foreigners who thought they could enjoy illegal smiles in a despot's police state? A clandestine peek downstairs a very long and dread-filled interval later revealed that the police were gone, and so were our passports. The desk clerk waved us off unconcernedly. He had made a handsome profit; the police could sell excellent copies of our documents to the highest bidder, and we were supporting the local economy. No jail time loomed, no imminent arrests. The relief left us positively giddy.

I was very happy to be sharing the room with my entourage of five, Malcolm, Kevin, Tony, Bob and Steve, all gallants after their own fashion. No one would be forcing the flimsy lock to ravish me during the night, a given had I been alone. This was not a four-star hotel, frequented by westernized Muslims or business travelers. It was a poor establishment in a run-down quarter of the city, where people lived according to ancient rules. It was certainly not customary for a woman to be without the protection of family, and if she were, she was probably a fallen woman available for the taking. A western woman alone would be viewed as doubly tantalizing.

Fortunately, my traveling partners were worldly enough to share a room or a bed with a woman without expectations of sexual reward. They even showered with me, allowing me relief from the searing heat while secure and defended. My companions got a chance to wash off the sweat of the day and feel manly and protective. I suppose they were also showing off for the sake of the locals, who never in their life would get to shower with an unmarried woman. I had learned early on that it was unsafe for me to walk the halls of the hotel alone. Every establishment had peepholes in the walls, and the spies were far from subtle. Even with an escort, I was at times accosted. Showering alone would have been inviting the devil to dance. Instead, I brought a friend, and we deliberately made a scene out of washing each other's hair or back. It drove the peeping ones wild, and never failed to bring exclamations and bumps against the walls as they jockeyed for better viewing position.

Sleep came slowly the first night in the flea bag hotel in Teheran. The lucky ones drifted off. The rest of us made quiet conversation as the hot winds blew across the peeling and shuttered windowsill, rustling the palms and wafting odors of burning oils and spice. Then the nightmare began. The first bed bugs to appear were reddish triangular ones with hard shells, which swarmed all over the unsuspecting sleepers. Next came little black ones, by the hundreds. Leggy gray insects followed. We were freaking out, knocking them off of ourselves as fast as we could manage, besieged, crazed, stoned, exhausted.

After a frantic hour, some gave it up. They wrapped their heads up in towels as best they could and rolled over, determined to sleep and shut out the assault. Tony and I watched the insects crawl on the faces of the unwary sleepers and enter their open mouths. It was a horror. Wave after wave of assault arthropods swarmed. I was burnt out from the heat, the travel, the relentless intensity of the men who tried to buy me, constant fears of assault, the threat of the police, and now the unwavering onslaught of vermin. I resolved to sit up all night, hands on my face, knocking bugs off. The lamp was turned down, burning dimly. Light shone under our door, illuminating the worn-out Persian carpet where we had sat earlier, appreciating the view. The creatures that came marching under the entry were truly borne of science fiction. Six to eight inches long, with multiple legs that elevated their dorsal regions several inches off the floor, they resembled transformers, giant scuttling cockroaches of horror film nuclear nightmares. I wanted to scream and cry, to make myself as small as possible, to bury myself inside my sleeping bag like a stork in the sand, making it all go away. Tony sighed and moaned and despaired with me, and finally gave it up, deserting me for sleep. Despite the heat and my fatigue, I sat up with the hood of my sleeping bag pulled over my head and knocked away creatures for hours. Scores of insects attempted to dive headlong inside. I flicked at every scuttle, dizzy and delirious. The night was endless, tortured, filled with infinite distress. Finally, I, too, slept.

The Amir Kabir hotel was a far superior establishment, an international watering hole for trekkers and adventurers, with only fleas hopping the sheets at night. I thought it to be an altogether satisfactory arrangement. It was two days before the last of the red bugs, burrowed deeply into our belongings, disappeared. The hotel was filled with dastardly attractive men, in their khakis and steel-toed boots, long telephoto lenses hanging from their gear. Nat Geo photographers in search of the perfect image, journalists, men on bold missions with impressive gear and the casual confidence of the explorer were everywhere. Intrepid adventurers with grit and guts, boldly trotting across the deserts and flirting with peril, their last encounter with a woman distant in the past. Females of the species were scarce out here, an unattached woman extremely rare. The plethora of voyagers, venturers, and wanderers of the male persuasion made my breath catch and my nether regions tighten from the intensity of their hot-eyed gazes. Not for the first time, there was a veritable feast laid before me, and it was Dom Perignon and filet mignon. I had to venture to the lobby carefully, acutely aware that my reality could alter irrevocably in an instant of compelling chemistry. I sat in wide-eyed contemplation in the room I shared in safety with the men I knew, whose presence was a necessity for my survival. They were stalwarts, safe, or so I thought then. Getting entangled in a new free-wheeling situation was not survival-smart on the planet's frontier. I would be risking my very life, but damn, it was hard to pass on chasing magic moments in a Land Rover roaming the Central Asian plateau. What to do?

With apologies to Robert Frost:

I am telling this with a sigh
In a faraway land ages and ages hence:
Two roads diverged in a desert wild
And sorry I could not travel both
long I stood
And looked down one as far as I could
Then took the other, the road more familiar.
And having perhaps the better claim,
Regret, I still ponder and look upon thy name....[4]

The BIT (British International Traveler) information guide warned of drug plants and setups. The police paid informants for tips so there was a lot of incentive for poor and nefarious types to falsely accuse foreigners. The most common scenario involved brushing against someone on the street and planting heroin or hashish on them, then having the police do a search and make the bust. That is exactly what happened to me on our way to the post office. A street urchin with an evil grin brushed full body against me and put a hand into the bag I was carrying. My companions drove him off angrily, and he ran. With my friends in a circle surrounding me, I took every article out of my bag. I could find nothing missing or added in. We were all shaken, this was the classic scene which didn't end well. After a thorough and fruitless search, we stopped at the post office on our way to the American Embassy to get visas for Afghanistan. The lines were long, governmental services were quite official in this part of the world and the bureaucratic procedures took a toll in patience.

A man burst into the building and ran up to the clerk behind the desk, speaking excitedly and gesturing. Suddenly they were both looking at me. The government official intoned in English, "May I see your bag, please?" "Give me your bag," said the spider to the fly. I nearly fainted. My legs were rubber. Mesmerized with fear, heart pounding from adrenalin and THC, I was handing over my bag before my brain could even begin to formulate an explanation. After more conversation in Farsi, the clerk begged my pardon. It seemed that the man who had come rushing in had seen me being accosted and was coming to my defense. He had chased down the perpetrator, had him held, and then found me. Was Madame all right? OMG. Madame was just peachy now that she had a reprieve from the firing squad. I did think that the actions of my would-be rescuer were exceptional and conveyed to him my many thanks. It was clearly time to get out of Dodge.

The American Embassy in Teheran was a walled compound with metal gates and a serene inner courtyard. It was a pleasant place, with busy workers at their desks and at atmosphere of calm efficiency. Overhead fans whirred a breeze and shade trees cast their cooling shadows. An oasis of reason and protection, it was located in the diplomatic quarter of Teheran, itself an enclave of sophistication and gentility. The hostage crisis, "Death to America!" and the Ayatollah Khomeini were just a few years away.

# Global

Chapter

# 5

# DASHT-I-KAVIR

There was no way east from Teheran without traversing the edge of the abyss. The Dasht-i-Kavir, the Great Salt Desert of Iran, loomed ominously in my path, one of the hottest and most uninhabitable places on earth. More than six thousand land miles lay behind me, past the ruins of Rome and Byzantium, through the dykes of the Netherlands and the oozing fogs of Oostende, across the dark Anatolian plain echoing with cries of crusaders wielding scimitars in the sun. Dasht-i-Kavir, abounding with diapirs and quicksand under its salt crusts, ringed by towering mountains, stalked by leopards and wolves in the darkness. By day, scorpions and poisonous lizards basked in its arid domain, parts of which have never known a single drop of rain. Hot, hot, burning hot, the earth below unsteady. Three of the largest seismic shifts in known history have struck here, in Bam and Ferdows and Manjil-Rudbar, tectonic strikes ramming rocks down the throats of tens of thousands and burying their human dreams forever in dust.

Abandon all hope, ye who enter here....[5]

Our strategy of continually moving east on local transport, picking up visas along the way, required rethinking. Alternative thinking which, as of yet, had yielded no options. Inquiries met resistance and shaken heads of dire warning, with no openings, no apertures for forward motion.

On the other side of the inferno lay Afghanistan, the land of hash and honey, and its Silk Road city of Herat. Legendary Herat, moated and gated, a fabled place of hanging gardens, the echoes of caravanserai hanging like dust motes in the air. Herat, a flower of Islamic hospitality, the goal of road-weary travelers on the overland trail from western civilization to the mysteries of the East. There was no airport, no train connections past the terminus of the Orient Express, some thousand miles westward in Istanbul. The road to paradise lay through hell.

Tony and Kevin greased palms enough to find us transport, a bus chock full of Pakistanis heading home after a migrant worker stint in Germany. It would be a four-day ride through the barren desert, a journey which pushed the envelope of visual perception. Rainbows arced across the sky, a backdrop to the austere barren beginnings of the Hindu Kush. All at once, the visual field included a vast expanse of empty desert, a background of disorienting oblique and vertical snowlines on the distant mountains, the black yurts of nomads, and the multi-colored layers of painted desert. Pink, green, orange, red and purple stripes stood out; stunning, vivid, bold. The Grand Canyon was bush league in comparison. This geological wonder of eastern Persia, modern day Iran, was created eons ago, and the corridor through it took one to the Silk Road, and the walled citadel of Herat. No one had told me there would be rainbows.

It was in ancient Persia that roses first bloomed, and nightingales sang. Astronomy was born to the Zoroastrians, who built blazing fire temples over ducts of natural gas. Mathematics was perfected here, and chess invented. Long before the Romans left Rome, the Persians had ruled an empire that stretched from the Indus to the Nile. It was four days hard ride in scorching heat and incessant motion. The bus stopped not. It would take us all the way from Teheran to Herat, six hundred miles distant, for fourteen dollars.

What we did not know until boarding was that conditions were already overcrowded, hostile, brimming with rage. We were unwelcome foreigners, symbolic of the indentured servitude of these men. The Pakistani workers had made extensive purchases with the wages of their labor in the west. Their precious goods were being carted back to families across the miles. Television sets and boxes of melamine dishes were stacked high across the seats. The driver led us to the piled-high rear of the bus with an ingratiating grin. How to carve out a space for six people? The passengers were territorial and hostile. Many had given up their seats so that their boxes of Western goods could ride in style. The driver began shifting cartons and very angry men came back to claim them, yelling and gesturing. They knew that the driver was making a few extra bucks for his pocket by taking us on and were enraged at the threat to the security of their hard-earned possessions.

Hairs rose on the back of my neck, the ancient arrector pili mechanism sensing primal danger. I was traversing these the badlands with five men, a testosterone drenched environment. And they were going. I was stuck, literally, between a rock and a hard box of melamine.

The passengers very grudgingly cleared room enough for about three people, at the insistence of the driver. Our party of six all squeezed together, and the bus took off, belching diesel fumes. The back windows were open and sucking in exhaust. Within a short time, we were sickened. We rolled around in our crammed seats, trying to alter the angle of the onrushing petrol-reeking wind, but it was a lost cause.

Hostilities soon broke out between several men over occupancy of the standing space on the rear stairs. They yelled loudly and menacingly at each other, displaying ruff, full of huff. The pushing began. Other passengers tried to calm them, to no avail, he who held the turf was bent on aggression. Amidst their shouting and shoving, a knife flashed out, silver arcing high to low as it plunged into soft space between hard ribs. The weapon, a blade about eight inches long, was withdrawn from the challenger's torso, as the stabber scrutinized nearby faces for further hints of intent. There were none forthcoming. As one, the men standing nearby lowered their heads and averted their gazes, the universal gesture of non-confrontation. The stabbed man quickly collapsed on a crate of dishes, nursing his bloody, dripping chest. The knife-wielder, triumphant, leering, held the space, the knife still menacing in his fist.

It was the seventh circle.[6] Fearing the Minotaur, I slunk low in my seat. Kevin flipped himself to lie underneath, body twisted, amidst boxes and garbage at people's feet. Tony and the others feigned sleep, breathing tersely. On we went, through the burning desert and disorder of our pathway to Herat. The bus ceased not, huge canisters of fuel on board, the dangers outside its confines more threatening than those within.

There was no English spoken, no universal language of international travel to be heard in this remote corner of terra firma. The meal stops were infrequent, and when they occurred, we were mystified. We ate the pita bread and onions, and ordered locally bottled drinks, a considerable risk but the only items of pseudo familiarity in sight. Not being able to communicate had major drawbacks, it was impossible to pantomime food specifics. The waiters at these road stops regarded us with a mixture of suspicion and condescension. Occasionally, they took us into the kitchens, but we could recognize nothing. We were hungry and losing weight, drinking chlorinated water and sugary soft drinks. The indoor plumbing of Teheran was a memory. Hot water and flush toilets had not been seen since Greece. There were no squatters or cesspits for either gender on the road. One time, feeling a particular urgency, I walked off to seclusion. I was preparing to squat when eight men emerged from the brush, wearing huge evil grins. Fortunately, I had asked my companions to stick close by and their combined presence managed to dissuade the jinns. Eventually, I had learned to nonchalantly urinate while standing up. This was accomplished after much trial and error. Without the option of underwear and, having burned my bras in a college rite of emancipation, my traveling garb was cotton and quickly managed. I wore a head scarf always, a paisley silk triangle that my father had brought home from England for his bride. To walk about without a head covering would have trumpeted my presence as a disrespecting infidel. Being a tall and fair young woman and was more than enough.

Somewhere in the Persian desert, a day east of Teheran, we were boarded by Iranian health officials. The uniformed men insisted that we take large red and white capsules immediately. Cholera had broken out in the nomad lands, and we were traversing the heart of the epidemic. Cholera? Our youth denied this as a possibility.

The uniformed officials stood by each seat with water and would not move on until they saw the pills go down. After the immediate dosage, a series of antibiotic capsules was suggested every four hours for several days. I did not want to comply. Who were these guys, really? Their antibiotics would upset my gut flora and only make me more vulnerable to the local enteric pathogens. Anyway, who knew what this shit was? Perhaps they had ulterior motives, to poison unwanted travelers. The health officials smiled but held their ground. I gauged how big a scene it would be if I refused. Watching the beady-eyed officials carefully assessing my friends and me, I concluded that there was no decision but to swallow. This was the Shah of Iran's police state, swallowing was the intelligent and expedient choice.

We went deeper and deeper into the mountains of eastern Persia. Seeing that empire firsthand, I could not call it Iran. Persia-lost empires of antiquity; a place where, denied alcohol, poetry became the intoxicant and aphrodisiac. I recalled traveling with my father to the Catskill Mountains, those aged and worn slopes formed by far gentler processes. I thought of the Alps, range upon range of sky-scraping stone peaks, majestic megaliths ultimately made homey and approachable by their European location. These mountains were alien, formed by massive collisions of the Arabian and Eurasian plates. The Elburz, the Aladaglar, the Roof of Khorasan, all these ranges had been thrust skyward by massive collisions, folded and subducted upon themselves. The mountains stood, multifaced and multifaceted, like clusters of rock crystal across a vista of burned-out desert, camels and sheep. Looking at their torturous formation, with peaks on every plane but the vertical, the snow outlining crevasses at impossible angles, caused in me a cognitive dissonance. They were too foreign, too unfamiliarly oriented, too impossible. I idly began to speculate that perhaps this place was not on my home planet. Had I fallen off a flat edge of the earth somewhere? What were the implications? Where was I? How did I get here? I longed for Afghanistan and the hanging gardens of Herat.

The Iran/Afghan border, on the Irani side, was much like its western border with Turkey. I remember glass display cases full of photos and paraphernalia of small-time drug traffickers, hapless westerner hippies, mostly, found with a kilo or a gram of hashish. Most of them were smiling, caught with the goods, expecting a year or two in jail at worst and a suspended sentence if lucky. The Lady had not smiled upon them. Next to the photos were index cards with their sentences. Life imprisonment, thirty years. The underground newspaper out of London had urged travelers to visit these people in their cells, to bring them soap, food, language, hope. We discussed the possibility, wanting to aid these unfortunate overlanders who had met such harsh fates in their travels. Ultimately, we thought ourselves to be in too much danger to enter Irani jails and exit without incident. I felt especially vulnerable as a female. Afghanistan was calling. Our visas in our pockets, we moved on.

We made the Afghan border too late in the evening to cross. This was a dilemma. Hotel rooms were available for the inflated price of forty dollars, an outrageous sum in that place, in that time. Indeed, in the entire nine months of my journey, I spent only $1500, including airfare from New York. Camping out on the Afghan border was met with dire predictions. It seemed that the local bandits were cutthroats, quite literally. We were advised to keep our valuables at the foot of our sleeping bags. Thieves could then slit open the bags while we slept and leave our persons untouched. It was only if they could not find your valuables that they did the throat-slitting. Thinking this was tongue-in-cheek propaganda put out by hotel scalpers, I watched the locals' body language and facial expressions, the only cues one could go by when language was such a barrier. Too many people walked by shaking their heads in obvious disapproval. "Stick together at all times," was pantomimed repeatedly.

My all-male road partners were offended and righteous at this imputed insult to their masculinity. They certainly were not about to be ripped off by anyone playing us for fools. They weren't about to spend the forty dollars, either. We made our encampment on a flat area of hard ground, apparently serpent and scorpion-free, a small distance from the border station. It was far away enough to force any would-be attackers into the open, and close enough for a survivor to run for help. That is, if there were any survivors. The Afghan tribesmen were legendary for their ferocity. A secret part of me would have liked the comfort of the hotel room, but I would not indulge that. It was I who would be taken, after all, disappearing into the desert for the pleasure of the local chieftain. Traveling with testosterone had some disadvantages. Not only was I the sole target, but I also had no one else to back up my point of view. As the lone female, I had to call up my yang reserves and tough it out. And I did.

We lay in a circle with our heads together and our feet radiating out like the spokes of a wheel. While the others made small talk, I decided to change the film in my Nikon. The film was stuck, there was no light but starlight, and I was nervous. I yanked. The entire shutter mechanism fell into my hands. In furious frustration, I put my ruined Nikon in the bottom of my sleeping bag with my passport and my money.

In the star-lit blackness, every shadow was a potential threat, every sough of the wind suspicious. We lay unsleeping and my bladder began to call. Tony let out a cry as I unzipped my sleeping bag, the mechanical noise loud in the darkness. He was sweetly full of anxiety for me as I crawled from our protective circle into the darkness. Tony again called out when he thought I had gone too far away. So much for stealth if there were bandits and so much for privacy from the five men who lay with bated breath in anticipation of my imminent death.

I fell asleep instantly when I crawled back into my bag. Morning came. Allah hu Akbar.

Chapter

6

☰

# THE WALLED CITADEL OF HERAT

**B**ells rang, echoing off the mountains, chiming down the broad boulevards of the ancient Silk Road city of Herat. White horses, their manes lovingly braided with red tassels and chimes, pulled silken carriages along the wide avenues. A wonder of the ancient world, seven-walled and moated Herat was renowned for its hanging gardens before the age of Persian emperors. The horses clopped a lively rhythm, their bells ringing, pulling the colorful carriages while men in flowing robes stood on platforms of old oil drums, directing traffic with whistles. Even the sunlight seemed less harsh.

All the mighty military names of Asian antiquity have passed through Herat; Alexander, Darius, Tamerlane, Chengiz Khan and others who conquered but never completely obliterated the famous city of the Silk Route. Chengiz Khan supposedly killed one and a half million people when he razed the city. After the survivors came creeping out of the ruins, he sent back his minions to slaughter them. Tamerlane's descendants rebuilt the city, but the British blew it up in 1888, in preparation for a feared Russian invasion.

The day that the U.S. invaded Afghanistan, I looked up high into the sky over New York and saw squadrons of military aircraft flying east. My heart sank. The New York skies had been no stranger to military operations since 9/11, but in my heart, I knew those planes were eastward bound for the land of deserts and dreams. Did my Afghanistan still exist? Had it been destroyed by the Soviets and then the emergence of the Taliban from the Pushtun? This enduring land has suffered many an arrogant conqueror throughout the ages. Poor and battered, Afghanistan has stood, its indomitable spirit of earth and fire triumphant, breaking the back of some of the empires that tried to destroy it.

The plain of Herat lay historically within the Persian Empire. Persian architecture could still be seen in Herat City in 1975, remnants of the five gates which had once graced the elevated walls. Alas, of the fabled moat, I saw no trace. The people spoke Farsi (or Dari Persian) as opposed to the Pushtu of the south and east of the country. I could hear the differences in the cadences as we traveled, but language remained a significant barrier.

Fortunately, the currency was nationalized and somewhat consistent with the Persian. The symbol for five was still a heart, and I had learned to read the number symbols from right to left a thousand miles ago.

Saffron, silks, fruit, and grain dominated the markets, although carpets were king. I was told by the merchants that the first wife a man bought was a skilled carpet maker, so that she could ensure his fortune. Electricity, like cars, was a rare thing. Men gathered by the light of kerosene and oil lamps in the evenings at the chaikanas, to drink from steaming samovars and eat flat bread cooked on griddles on the ground. I was not welcome, of course, being female. Only men were allowed at public gatherings or eating places. Still, the scrutiny here was far less intense than I had endured in Turkey or Iran. The relief of just being an infidel not worthy of much notice was considerable. I wished there were other women to interact with, local women, but they did not enter the public sphere.

In the afternoons, we hired a carriage, pulled by the magnificent gawdis, the paired horses, for a ride up into the mountains to watch the sun set on the Silk Road. The roundtrip took a couple of hours and cost thirty cents. Most of the horses were white, with an occasional pair of grays. Their manes, woven with the red silk pompoms and ever-chiming bells, and the carriages, lined with multicolored silks, created an atmosphere of festivity. When we hired a carriage in the late afternoons, no mobs or street hustlers accosted us in this non-urbanized, still nomadic nation. No heads turned; no calculating schemers plotted to separate us from our dollars. As a group of kaffirs, we were mildly amusing, unimportant, and left to our own devices. It was euphoric.

My loose coalition of foreign friends survived well into Herat. We found a hotel with amenities, color-coordinated mattress pads and pillows upon the rope beds. The charpoy was the standard in Afghanistan, a frame of tightly bound ropes set on legs. Mattresses, and bedding in vibrant colors, were simply unknown. The fact that these innovations had never been washed did not dismay us. We were seasoned overlanders, not tourists flying in for a few days on another planet. We wanted to experience firsthand the conditions of diverse cultures and ways of life before they were westernized and industrialized out of existence. My years as a social worker in the bowels of Manhattan and the Bronx had left me empty and in search of meaning. "New York, yes, yes, very good place," could be heard in Afghanistan, but that was in Kabul, the capital, and ancient Herat had almost no English speakers beside the merchants. I felt no Soviet presence, even though the Russians had a railhead only 50 miles north in Kushk.

Like much of Asia, this was not a place for nightlife, the pulse of activity occurred during the day. Sunrise began the busy start of the daily exertions. Evenings brought a leisurely meal and conversation. The

Prophet had frowned upon music and there was a dearth of it in this world. Still, it was possible to hear the haunting sounds of harmoniums and tambouras in the western cafes that catered to the flower children. The restaurant owners were more than accommodating, and even provided singers of melancholy voice projected from the throat, not the diaphragm.

California Bob appeared in one of the cafes, a tall, long-haired Jewish boy from Beverly Hills, riding a giant Harley alone across the desert. Wherever he went on that bike, he was a magnet for the testosterone set. Afghan boys swarmed him, grinning, petting the bike reverently. Bob was literate, gentle, bearded, and looked like a Biblical prophet. I loved his conversation, and his Harley wasn't bad either. I was free, but California Bob wasn't. Although he escorted me to the restaurants and bazaars, there was too much talk about the girl he left behind in LA. Philadelphia Bob, headed east to India, remained steadfast. He was young, about 21, and on his virgin voyage outside of the familiar confines of U.S. His innocence often embarrassed me, and I could have been far more tolerant of his unsophisticated American mannerisms and lack of international cool. Alas, I was seven years older, in possession of a passport thick with stamps and just had too many notches in my belt. PA Bob continued swilling sugary drinks and pining for a semblance of the American familiar all along the Asian trail while his sugar-rich, B vitamin-deficient blood remained a magnet for mosquitoes. He scratched and moaned and mourned the dearth of lemonade. As a self-righteous vegan, I was disciplined, renunciate, and not tasty to the biting hordes.

Marco Polo traveled the length of Afghanistan in the 1200s, following the Oxus River. Familiarly referred to as "Marco" by the locals, who all had grandfathers who knew him, I thought they were referring to an Italian hippie! I learned to drink chai in Herat, hunkered down in a squat in a merchant's booth in the bazaar. All business was conducted on one's haunches, and soon it became second nature. Hot chai was sweetened by holding a mint candy behind your front teeth until the hot liquid dissolved it. Unfortunately, it dissolved the teeth too. Huge cavities between the front incisors were common, dental care unknown.

The men of the bazaar vied for our attention, conversation, and business. In choosing a particular merchant, you were accepting his network or brothers, "cousins" and friends who would provide for your every need. His wives and mother would sew your clothing to order. As an American of primarily Celtic descent by way of Scandinavia, I was a whole lotta woman for that part of the world. This aroused no end of giggles from the merchants. The first time I was shown to a changing room, I accommodated by removing most of my clothing until I realized that Abdullah was going to stay and check me out, in frank and titillated appraisal. Fortunately, these Herati merchants were a softer breed than their Turkish or Iranian counterparts and I had no immediate fear of rape. I never went to the bazaar without a male escort, however, and more than one if I could manage it. Abdullah worked hard to convince me to go to the Hilton hotel for a swim in the pool, a favorite afternoon diversion of his fellow semi-affluent shopkeepers. Declining, I did provide him with a studio photo for his collection. The walls of the merchants' shops were a fascinating array of passport pictures, photos of the flower power of western youth looking off into the unknown. I wondered what strange fate brought all of us to this place at this time as Abdullah added my face to the mix.

One afternoon, Abdullah took me into the back room of his shop. Shelves lined three of the four walls, from floor to ceiling. Canisters crowded each shelf, large containers, each of which could hold at least the equivalent of five pounds. He took one down and opened it for me, showing me the yellowish, powdery contents. Kief, the THC-rich golden resin of the marijuana plant. It was collected in the mornings by the local farmers, who walked through the fields in leather aprons, which the sticky sap would coat. When an apron was suitably covered, it was removed and the resin scraped off. Dried resin was pressed into cakes of hashish. No wonder the average purchase of hash here was a kilo, 2.2 pounds! Abdullah's shop alone must have contained 500+ kilos of kief. I saw no evidence of opium or poppies, but knew the fields were zealously guarded by rifle-wielding guards. By 2007, the conversion of many poppy fields to cannabis was common in response to crackdowns on the heroin trade. Allegedly, this increased the profits for the Afghan farmers.

The hotels in Herat had a welcoming amenity, not chocolates or fancy soap, but a half ounce of hashish per guest. The common rooms were lovely, with rich cushions scattered on thick carpets, wall textiles, and even hookahs for your delight. One factor that was no different here, however, was the maddening and demonic pursuit of my flesh. The constant question was of the truth of my marital status. The hotel staff could not figure out which of my traveling companions was my husband. That I might be unattached never entered their consciousness. It was unfathomable. I watched the petite women on the streets in their chadris, navigating in the head-to-toe tent-like garment with dense netting over their eyes. Usually, four women followed one man down the street, only the tips of their little plastic shoes peeking out enticingly. Silent and seemingly subservient, they maintained a respectful distance behind their husband and did not talk amongst themselves. The sister wives had a hierarchy and structured roles, and while jealousies and rivalries were common, so was acceptance. The woman's place was in the home, cared for and protected by her husband.

As a witness to women's liberation and the humanistic social movements of the 1970s, my intrigue and fascination alternated with outrage. What power did women really have? The Prophet says it is a man's duty to please his wife, and so perhaps the male had to privately meet expectations for his wife's sexual satisfaction. Women seemed to appreciate being sheltered from intrusive male gazes and commentary. Adhering to the dress code and donning the head-to-foot chadri or burka granted anonymity and respect, but it was not enough for freedom of the streets. Outside of the home, a woman must always be accompanied by a male family member as well as modestly concealed under the tent. Women who did not follow these norms were viewed as not respectable by both men and other women. I dressed modestly for a westerner, a skirt to mid-calves, a long-sleeved shirt over my tank top, my small headscarf as a token to propriety. My instincts, however, were those of a single, adventurous, liberated female immersed in a medieval land of exotic sights, sounds and smells. Men were on my radar. Despite my antagonism to the customs, an instinct for caution and an anthropologist's desire not to offend mores, I could not help but notice the dark and handsome males who roamed the bazaar. One late afternoon, I saw a regal man in gray embroidered silk silhouetted against the westering sun. A gentle breeze billowed his robes and displayed his proud posture. He had large liquid Tajik eyes and neat moustaches; no wives followed in his footsteps. Could I? Could a western woman entertain a casual dalliance with an Afghan warrior and walk away? I mulled the prospect for several days, catching his eye in the bazaar. Casual eye contact became lingering gazes. We spoke not a word, but conversation bloomed in body language. I contemplated the possibilities. Lifting a chadri in the bazaar, I noticed its considerable weight and the engulfing nature of its design. The chadris then were almost always black, silk, and impossibly difficult in the searing heat. I thought of buying one for the phenomenal party costume it would make, but I couldn't get past the subservience it represented. I decided to try one on. As it descended over my head, I lost my breath in the billowing blackness. It threatened to engulf me, cloaking me in isolation and dependence. Vision was obstructed by the network of fabric that covered the eyes. I dropped the garment, singed.

I favored the nomad dress, bright red, flowered, and spangled with glittering silver coins. Were nomad women freer than their citified sisters? It would seem so from their dress. The nomad women veiled their mouths and covered their hair, but the sight of them in their red dresses and layers of heavy silver jewelry, black eyes heavily kohled, suggested compelling sexuality and female mysteries of great allure. The heaviness of the dresses, covered with metal coins, was just too much weight to carry for a journeyer who needed mobility. With real regret, I let go of the red dresses and my inner dancing woman of the desert sands. Traveling light was where it was at. The coolest of world travelers carried only a small leather bag with a change of clothes and a book

In conversation with the merchant Abdullah, I learned the way of marriage in Herat in 1975. An aspiring young man would work hard for three or four years to save the money for a wife. His work was constant, without benefit of time clock, vacations, or weekends off. When he had finally amassed enough coin, he purchased his first wife, a widow perhaps twenty years his senior. As an experienced rug maker, she would earn him enough in a year or two to follow his loins to spring pastures. The family of the first wife would be happy to be rid of a burden. The woman, it was inferred, would be happy to have a husband and a home. At forty she could be a crone, often toothless, haggard, and depending on the charity of unwilling others. She had few possessions, and no status unless it was derived from a man. Once widowed or rejected, women were desperate for remarriage to provide a roof over their heads, food, and relief from the abhorrently shameful status of being a woman without a man.

Girls attended school in Herat until the age of fourteen. Uniformed, fresh-faced, unveiled and virgin, they left school in the afternoons in little groups, aware of but ignoring the hungry-eyed men lurking at the shops nearby. A lucky man who negotiated well got to take one of these beauties home as wife, wrapping her in the veil of purdah behind sunbaked walls. Soon she would be joined by another, and if he were very successful, wife number four joined the household.

I took tea in the hotel's common room, contemplative on the cushions. The hotel owner had a Tajik cap, the big liquid eyes, and favored caftans of blue.

His younger brother, more westernized, wore tight short pants and spoke some English. The establishment had the ubiquitous peep holes in the shower room, for an intimate view of nude western women, and perhaps nude men too. One day, Younger Brother made the dreaded accusation: "I have heard that you are not married!" An unmarried woman was an outrage, an affront, a liability, an invitation. This woman, unmarried by choice and steeped in early feminist ideology, was feeling too strongly the effects of overwhelming genderist stress. I threw caution and mores to the winds. I had five male traveling companions. "Yes, I am married," I informed him, "they are all my husbands!" He erupted in fury, scandalized, inferring that an unmarried woman traveling with men was their whore. I wouldn't have baited him further if he had not been so disagreeable, so avaricious, a grifter dealing drugs from his brother's legitimate hotel, spewing anti-female rhetoric. I held the position that all of the men I traveled with were husbands of mine, available at any time for satisfaction of my whims. He sputtered, spraying saliva, incensed, enraged. He continued to harangue me bitterly and the next day, and I hit upon a solution. The charpoys were wide enough for two. For a few nights, I moved from bed to bed, settling in for sleep with a different guy; just friends, no benefits. I was making a point. It left my Afghani tormentor speechless. In my country, women are free to have as many men as they choose.

The shower room had an overhead tank and a spigot. The tank was filled several times a day with water carried on the back of the hotel laborer. This strapping young man from the provinces carried the water and did the general maintenance on the premises. He was kind and gentle by nature and quietly fascinated by us. His duties included being mistreated by my aforementioned antagonist, delivering food, and manning the heavy gates of the establishment, which were closed at darkness. He was on call throughout the night to open the gates for late arrivals who stayed out at the cafes. By day, he labored ceaselessly in the hot sun. It was usually between 100- and 110-degrees F that early summer in Herat, dusty and flyblown.

One late afternoon we returned to the screams of a French guest. She stood upon her bed watching two large scorpions battle to the death. The gentle–souled laborer, Mohammed, killed them with a stick. Two days later, he did a similar deed for me. I was sitting with Kevin on his charpoy, enjoying chai in the shade of the courtyard. As I set my cup down on his mattress, it unbalanced and spilled. Full of apologies, I sat up as he patted his mattress, felt bumps, and lifted it to investigate. He jumped like an NBA all-star, emitting a frightened scream. The dun-colored scorpion was four or five inches long, stinger erect. Mohammed again came to the rescue, ultimately stomping it to death. All in a day's work. When he got paid, he sent most of the money back to his mother and sister in the provinces. His salary was twenty dollars every year.

When hell broke loose in the form of dysentery, it was Mohammed who nursed us. He got the doctor from the Red Crescent station, who prescribed no food for four days and sips of liquids, when we could stand the pain of drinking them. Trouble had reared its head the first night in Herat. Several restaurants advertised in simple English or French that they served only water boiled for a half hour. We chose one. Returning to the hotel, a flat-roofed, dried mud structure, we heard deep, agonizing groans. The sounds came from what was euphemistically called the WC, or water closet. The squatters were pits, open holes in many places. Here at the hotel, the structure was a six-foot-wide room with a trench dug on a 45-degree angle for about twelve feet. The slide looked to be of concrete but was really just hardened mud like most of the local construction. Also hardened upon it were streams of excrement of various colors and states of liquidity. There were kilos and kilos of old fecal matter, with current deposits layered on top. A brass water pitcher sat at the right side of the slide. We had learned "pour with your right, wipe with your left," many kilometers past and only occasionally presented our suspect left hands at table. Actually, the practice was far cleaner than toilet paper for the nether regions and upon consideration made our tree-killing paper use seem unhygienic and barbaric. The problem remained that left hand. Antiseptic wipes and hand cleaner were decades in the future, heated bathing water unknown, and a squeaky clean behind resulted in a contaminated left hand. There were bidets in even the simplest of hotels, but unfortunately these were often mistaken for more common plumbing. "Stupid Americains, this in non a toilette" was a furious epigraph found on one squatter wall. The Ugly American, even off-planet.

We became very ill. Our tongues swelled and turned bright yellow, sticking to the roofs of our mouths. The vomiting and diarrhea were uncontrollable, with weakness, fever, even delirium. Accidently spying my reflection, I was shocked by the purple rings under my eyes and the overall wasted appearance. Trips to the squatter were fraught with the real possibility of toppling head first into the cesspit morass. And trips we made, as many as twenty or thirty a day. Complicating matters were the infernal black flies. The din of thousands of buzzing insects only quieted with the sunset. First light brought hordes of biters flying in your mouth and up your nose. And at squatting time, they were merciless. If you yelled when they stung your delicate, exposed privates, they would fly into your open mouth before you could get it shut. Cierra la boca! Ferme la port!

We suffered and moaned and sweated and slept when we could. All six of us were incapacitated. The local doctor now suggested eating opium. It caused projectile vomiting and complete disorientation. The carpet I lay on lifted, and airborne, circled Herat. Dusty, sunbaked, barren, parched, foreign, unbearably exotic Herat. We vomited, moaned, vomited, shit, and dreamed of home. Home was a different place for all of us, with holidays in common and other holidays unique and unknown. Most of us were unable to eat. Dehydrated, I craved water so badly but the pain of drinking it made me scream. I could not stop my swallowing mechanism, blissful water streaming down my parched throat. I knew I would pay as it hit my stomach, but my throat was in command and I swallowed, only to vomit again. Was it typhoid? Cholera? What was that mystery medicine that we were forced to swallow in Iran?

Mohammed, bless his soul, fetched water for me. He insisted, by gesture, that I let him bathe my feet. It was an unabashedly religious experience. I felt like the woman at the well. His dedication and willingness to care for us were moving. Gradually, we started to recover. Malcolm, the first one to get ill, began to stabilize. Kevin was second, followed by Tony. As we lay abed too weak to move, we fantasized about our favorite holiday foods. Lamb and mint jelly for the Kiwis, turkey and trimmings for the Americans, blood puddings for the Brit. Malcolm told stories of Aussie social gatherings, routinely segregated by gender. American cultural icons such as Superman were discussed in detail with foreigners who considered themselves expert on the story of the anti-Kryptonite man but had never heard of Jimmy Olsen or Perry White. I denied the possibility of kangaroos routinely hopping down the road on the street where you live. Hilarity set in, endorphins crashing around our fever-battered brains, we held onto our bellies, now aching from gut-wrenching laughter. We were alive, we would survive. We were on the road again. Onward!

California Bob, a frequent visitor, was also ready to hit the trail. He came by with a proposal one of our last days in Herat. It seemed that he wanted to ride his Harley near our bus, pace himself with us as we headed out, keep a friendly eye on each other. My Afghan pseudo dalliance forgotten, I wanted to jump on the back of his Harley, wrap my arms around him, and take off into the unknown. I wanted to know the taste of his kisses and the feel of his body and the sounds and textures of him. He was strangely reluctant. I pressed a bit, he demurred. He finally told me that he had the shits so badly that he couldn't control himself. He was worried about falling off the bike and dying somewhere in a ditch. I couldn't ride behind him; I might be blown off the bike!

Before we left Herat, I had a plan. The coolest of international travelers needed just a small bag, not a backpack. There was a huge demand for American jeans, at that time worth thirty dollars on the black market. There were six of us, some with more than one pair of extra jeans. We also had shirts, books, shoes, jewelry, pens, expensive camping gear and assorted other western paraphernalia. Mohammed got it all. He sat on the bed in our room and sobbed. The tears streamed down his cheeks, covering his hands, running to his elbows. Removing the silver bangle from his wrist, he held it out to me in offering. The clothing and gear we gave him was probably worth twenty-five years of hotel wages.

I like to think of him still. Did he go home to his mother and sister? Perhaps he got his own shop and brought the family to the city, eventually becoming a prosperous merchant. Did he survive the Russians? Is he alive now? As salaam aleiykum, Mohammed. It was my honor.

Chapter

# 7

# RAGE OF PURDAH

"Now I see the secret of the making of the best persons.
It is to grow in the open air and to eat and sleep
with the earth." [7]

WALT WHITMAN, *Song of the Open Road*

Qandahar or Mazar? This was the choice upon leaving Herat, Afghanistan's ancient, walled, silk route fortress. Mazar-i-Sharif was the legendary resting place of Ali, regarded by the Shiah to be the Prophet's rightful successor. His city lay on a pilgrimage path to the north and east of Herat. To go north was to journey through rugged terrain near the Soviet border with transportation only by truck, and that, with luck. The lake district of Afghanistan, an unheralded wonder of the world, also lay north and east, vast volcanic calderas on a parching plain. Their rims arched to touch the sky, elevated thousands of feet above the plains. The Afghans told that the lakes were bottomless. Photos showed raised rock chalices, desert barren of life forms or trees, just sere xeriscape and lipped rocky brims reaching for the heavens amidst achingly blue skies.

The lure of the Silk Road was considerable, Mazar-i-Sharif legendary. The merchants would shake their heads in wonder and awe each time they spoke of it. The statues of Sakyamuni still stood then in the Bamiyan Valley, a testament to the spread of Buddhism across Asia into China a millennium and a half before. The Taliban found these ancient monuments so perturbing they dynamited them in a tragic offense against world heritage. For me, they stood, carved, immutable, calling. I thought I might loop from Mazar-i-Sharif to the Bamiyan Valley and enter Kabul from the northwest instead of the south, completely avoiding Qandahar.

The problem with this plan was the lack of roads. I could follow the Oxus River, as Marco Polo had done, seven hundred years before. Or I could attempt to penetrate the rugged central mountain region of the Hazarah. I found the Hazarah faces fascinating, with their high cheekbones, epicanthal folds, and lack of facial hair. These men wore heavily embroidered skullcaps instead of turbans and were instantly recognizable for their features as well as their dress. Hazarahs are considered to be descendants of the Mongol conqueror, Chengiz Khan. He left thousand-man military units, the hazars, behind him on his westward push through the territory to find the glories of Persia. They were considered low caste among the Afghans, their lands barren, remote, almost waterless. They are also Shiahs, a minority in a country 90% Sunni. Many left their desolate homelands to find their fortunes as laborers in the cities. I came to learn that there was no real passage through the Hazarajat except on horseback.

Uzbekistan and Turkmenistan loomed above northern Afghanistan. The border ran along the Oxus for more than a thousand miles. In eastern Iran, I had witnessed barbed wire fences and stark gun towers manned by Soviet soldiers, spanning the border for hundreds of miles. The people on the Soviet side of the wicked wire fences looked poor and downtrodden compared to their Afghani and Irani counterparts. Transportation could not be guaranteed for the four- or five-day trek to Mazar. It was a sacred city, although infidels did visit, they were few and undesirable to the Muslim faithful. The Hindu Kush lay in earnest between Mazar and Kabul, gateway to the Khyber Pass and the east. Qandahar, south of Herat, was a mere eighteen-hour journey. My third choice, directly across the remoteness of Hazarajat on horseback, would be an adventure of stunning proportions. But would it be survivable? I was recovering from a dysentery unimaginable to my previous American mindset. Another round of that out in the Afghan wilderness could easily prove my demise. As captivating and stirring as I found Afghanistan, I wanted to live to tell about it. Lions once roamed here, free and noble. I felt inexplicable stirrings of homeland in this raw and magnificent place, but I knew I had other horizons to conquer. And might I not be captured, an exotic concubine in a burning desert yurt? I opted for the more cautious travel plan, though my inner adventurer wailed. Decades later, after having the family DNA run, I learned that my father's forebears, heavily Denisovan, had spent millennia wandering in Central Asia tens of thousands of years ago. The ancient echoes still resonated in my DNA.

Avoiding the Wardak bus company, known to strand travelers in the desert, my intrepid trail buddies and I climbed aboard a shiny small vehicle for the trip to Qandahar. Fortune soon deserted us. The bumper of the bus, sturdy and in normal alignment when we left Herat, seemed to become molten and accordion in upon itself. The heat was ferocious, and I like to think it had just melted the damn thing. If the air temperature was more than 110 degrees, how hot was that bumper, with the sun reflecting on it and the heat from the engine and the road below factored in? It was rubbing on the front left tire and soon made operating the truck impossible. Our driver and his stalwarts, after whacking at the bumper with various implements, nursed the vehicle to a little chaikana a couple of hours out in the desert. Then they climbed aboard a loud little panel truck and roared away, with no ceremony but sincere promises of return. I watched the faces of the men at the teahouse carefully. There were no smirks, no traces of cruelty, just nodding heads and gestural assurances that the entourage would soon return to our rescue.

Something else was coming too, and it didn't look good. The sky darkened and men rapidly began stowing items inside the little chaikana, a 10 by 12-foot mud hut. They unwound their turbans, covering their faces, mouth, nose, and eventually, eyes. We were gestured to get down low and we did. The sandstorm hit with a loud voice, ululating like the women of this desert land. It blasted my face with stinging sand, sharp and cutting as shards of glass. Scarf pulled over mouth and nose was woefully inadequate. Wind tore at my eyelids, blasting grit so fast and furiously that I had to rip off the scarf and bandage my eyes with it. I worked the fabric over my face with my hands, eventually covering eyes and nose. Mouth clamped shut, breathing through my covered nostrils as shallowly as possible, I huddled on the ground with my back to the wall of the chaikana, knees drawn up to protect my face while howling, biting dark chaos ruled the known world.

There were sounds all around us, muted by the pandemonium of nature, yet discernible. Things were falling off the flat roof of the building, hitting the ground near us with a plopping sound. Plop plop plop plop, noises everywhere, and sensations of being brushed against. Malcolm, now my romantic partner, crawled off in the pitch darkness of the howling maelstrom to scream a question in the ear of the nearby Afghans. I didn't like it when he left me, and I liked it less when he returned. I could feel the taut intensity of his body as he settled back beside me. Scorpions, their sunbath on the roof of the chaikana disrupted, were raining down around us like hailstones from hell. We huddled our bodies as close together as possible, trying to cover ourselves with the flesh of the other. There was nothing to do but to wait it out. I tried not to think about the huge, dun colored Afghani scorpions, four to five inches long, with deadly erect stingers.

The storm wailed and lashed at us, shrieking in an unknown voice. It was a female voice, of dark awe-ful power and terror. Was it this primal generative power so feared that women were locked away behind centuries-old walls? Muslim, Christian, Jew, each Abrahamic sect had its history of censoring female sexual and reproductive power. In this desert, every village seemed a fortress, walled and slotted. Misogyny was endemic here long before Islam took root a thousand years ago. Was the rage of Purdah the voice of this primal chorus? It seemed so.

After what seemed like hours, the storm abated. It could literally have been hours, time was reckoned only by the sun, and sol's disc was obscured. None of the Afghans wore the status symbol watch; we were supercool overland travelers who shunned the symbols of a lost world. We waited for the rest of the day, chastened and diminished by this raw power we had witnessed. Just before dusk, our charioteers returned, brimming with smiles, in a rusty old bus belching exhaust. Gratefully we climbed aboard; hungry, hurting, pummeled, exhausted, beaten up, broken down, messed up, molested, whipped, and wiped out. We sat drooping in our seats on the crowded bus, filled to capacity as it pushed through the blackness of the desert. The night held other terrors. Our dozing was suddenly interrupted as the bus jerked to a stop, surrounded by soldiers. They came out of the darkness of night and boarded us, rifles at the ready. Their rifles were wooden, old Enfield's, with deadly bayonets fixed. They began demanding papers and forcibly evicting protesting men from their seats, men who declaimed their innocence in more and more frantic terms. I watched from the back of the bus, secure in my American semi-divinity and my youth.

The soldier with his bayonet in my face was no more than eighteen. He seemed barely verbal and his gaze was vague, unfocused. His gray uniform, Soviet issue, was ripped at the collar. Taking my passport, he read it upside down. I wanted to laugh as this skinny dude stood fumbling through my documents. I had little respect for his culture's treatment of women, I was fresh from college campuses where burning bras was a rite of emancipation. The moment came when my picture in the passport oriented him and he realized his error. His now piercing gaze, assessing my reaction, was dead-eyed cold. A greater wisdom prevented the laughter that had bubbled up, as a chill ran down my spine. I gazed blankly over his shoulder, not meeting his eyes. He continued staring for several years, watching me closely. I did not take a breath until he had moved on. The men pulled off the bus in the blackness of that night were never seen again.

Afghanistan's longest peace prevailed from 1931, with the departure of the British and the establishment of a constitution; until 1973, when Muhammed Daud seized the reins of government. Daud, the former Prime Minister and cousin to the royal family, was a professional soldier with strong ties to the Russian-trained military and a personal grudge about the Pushtun issue. The Pushtuns, or Pathans as they were formerly known, held ancestral lands which were cleaved in two by the infamous Durand Line, which established the borders between Afghanistan and its neighbors Russia to the north, Iran to the west and Pakistan to the east. It was Britain and Russia who drew these borders, establishing administrative districts for the superpowers and dividing the ancestral Pushtun lands in two. Had the Durand fiasco, with its remarkable lack of sensitivity to tribal history and concerns, not occurred, the fate of the region would have followed a far different path. The U.S. allied with Pakistan after its creation in 1947, refusing to economically support Afghanistan because of the Pushtun issue and shutting the Afghan/Pakistan border to trade. This had serious economic consequences for the fledgling Afghan economy and led to its reliance upon aid from the Soviet Union. The Soviet Prime Minister Khrushchev pledged support for Pushtun autonomy in 1955, fueling hopes of an independent Pushtunistan. Crafty Khrushchev backed up his talk with a $100 million low interest loan and the stage was set for rerouting Afghan trade to the north and a Soviet sphere of influence. Eventually the Soviets invaded to "stabilize" the Afghan civil war, a disaster for both countries. The Afghan/Pakistan border continues to remain porous, hiding Osama bin Laden's armies after 9/11 and serving as the site of radical Islamic training camps to this day.

There were fifty-eight Afghanis to the dollar in 1975, purple and plastered with Daud's visage. This eighteen-hour ride would cost one hundred of them. I don't remember a road per se, just endless track of hard-baked desert and rugged mountains. The heat was relentless and nomads were everywhere, 80% of the population was still nomadic. The women blazed brightly in their brilliant red dresses and glinting metal jewelry, their faces speaking of Chenghiz Khan and lost empires. The chadri or burkah was not seen here, though many faces were veiled to the eyes. It was the faces turned away from us, veiling loosened in the heat, which spoke so eloquently.

Camels and flocks of fat-tailed sheep were a constant impediment. One had to develop a certain relationship with the animals while crossing these lands. We traveled by motor, and it was rare to see any other vehicles but the gaudily painted Afghan panel trucks, and those were an unusual sight outside of the cities. Humans rode camels and horses and got about on foot. The camels were large and loopy-gaited, riddled with mange and patches of missing fur. They had narrow faces and unpleasant expressions with thick curly eyelashes to protect against blowing sand. Chewing non-stop with their mouths open, they made rude noises and stank. Each fresh glimpse of camel meant another delay, as the men on their backs herded their flocks of sheep across our vehicle's path. Sheep had the right-of-way out here, and the delays could be a half hour long. Sometimes one flock would finally pass and we would start the engine, only to be shut down again five minutes later. The sheep were fat-tailed, oily, and bleating; black, white, and mixed. Their dung had a distinctive reek, and globules of sheep fat (and maybe sheep shit) continued to float on top of our nasty-tasting tea. Sheep ruled.

Qandahar, a city of the Pushtun, lay in the south above the Registan desert, most of which was uninhabitable. To the southeast fell the Durand line, dividing the Pushtun into Afghans and Pakistanis, and the two barren provinces of southern Pakistan. The nomads skirted the borders of these no-man's lands, driving their flocks to water on the fertile banks of the Arghandab River. Qandahar province was a land rich in agricultural wealth. It was renowned for its almonds, grapes, melons, and especially hashish and opium. We spent our first night there smashing open the shells of the petite almonds of the region with rocks, driven wild by their sweetness. In the morning, California Bob came by with four cans of Jaffa orange juice found in the bazaar. There were no can openers, and the thought of the taste, after weeks of living on bread and onions, was maddening. We finally slit open the cans with our knives and drank and drank again. I have never known a sweeter nectar in my life than the juice of those Jaffa oranges that June morning in Qandahar.

I remember white-washed walls, open courtyards, cobbled streets, turbaned men, women in chadors. It was a quiet town after Herat, newer, lacking the Silk Route mystique. There were several choices of hotels that catered to the backpacker set. The Peace Hotel, our choice, was a fine establishment which charged 15 Afghanis per night. The other possibilities, the Hotel Babe Waile and the Hotel Tourist, were unavailable during our month-long stay, perhaps because a big drug deal was going down. The plants that the Afghans harvested to make hashish grew in the streets of Qandahar. They were cultivated, not wild, and there as a sign of permissiveness. I never saw any Afghan using drugs, but the hippies were another tale. Red-eyed and dazed, they wandered the streets with the quintessential fabric shoulder bags hanging by their sides. The bags were neatly sized to hold a kilo, 2.2 pounds of hashish. In the immortal words of the balladeer John Prine, "You may see me tonight with illegal smile, it don't cost very much, but it lasts a long while...." [8]

It seemed that everyone slept under the stars in Qandahar, and we soon joined the practice. It was in Qandahar that I felt the natural rhythm of the earth's motion settle on me like a mantle. We rose every morning with the sun, usually before four a.m. The whole world woke then; the hordes of flies, the men crouched at their morning ablutions over the drainage ditches, the steaming samovars and hot griddles frying up breakfast. Bedtime came an hour or so after the sun went down, settled around a campfire. The Afghan men got out their Flit pumps before retiring, spraying their grassy sleeping areas with reckless glee. These were the old-fashioned hand-held spray pumps from the fifties in the U.S. I flashed on the halcyon days of my childhood, my grandparents' summer house in the pine groves of Long Island, my uncles' laughter on the air, the sun heating the pine sap to an olfactory inundation. Our turbaned friends obligingly offered to spray a patch of grass for me too. I had no fear of sharing the sleeping space; my guy friends were around me; I had a cozy sleeping bag on the earth, and the stars were a hundred million crystalline winking universes above me. I could recognize few constellations, tipped on their sides and oriented to an unfamiliar longitude on the far side of the planet as they were, and that only made the nights more magical. It was all so incomprehensibly vast.

I rose each morning with the sun. I had more energy than I had ever known, those brief days in tune with the circadian rhythms of planet earth, that Qandahar, that June.

Chapter

# 8

# KABUL

The big city was pancaked, layer upon layer of flat-topped adobe construction dominating its appearance. The ancient fortress of Ba'ala Hissar overhung the city, reminding the visitor that Kabul was standing when the angry Aryans swept by on their way to enveloping India. Clearing the Paghman mountains to the west, Kabul dominated the approaches to the Hindu Kush along the Silk Route.

The journey there from Qandahar, a trans-desert trek of several days in an ancient vehicle, was notable for the contact we had with two Afghan women. Sister wives, they traveled with their husband and their young son. They sat together, sewing and talking quietly, while the husband was seated with the boy of about eight. The sun burned through the windows of the bus. The temperature exceeded 100 degrees; the bright sky hurt the eyes. The women sat uncomplaining in their chadors, their faces and bodies draped in heavy black fabric. Eventually, one of the women pulled the small leatherette window curtain a few inches to the side to block the sun's rays. I had done the same, it really did make a difference to be shielded from the directness of the sun. The small boy, sitting with his frowning father behind the women, yanked the curtain back. The woman forbore his behavior with no reaction. A few minutes later, she tried again. He grunted and yanked the curtain back to a position suitable for him. The boy's head swiveled around the bus, a scowl on his face. I couldn't tell if he was looking for other passengers' reactions or if he was looking for other female perpetrators. A while later, the sun full bore in her eyes, the woman made another adjustment. The boy slapped her face, hard. There was a breathless moment, and then a hideous lack of reaction. The father looked bored and had no reprimand for his son's mistreatment. Not a single passenger commented or reprimanded that child. The woman said not a word. Her face was hidden under the chador, but she didn't look in the boy's direction, react to what was obviously a painful slap, or in any way protest. This was doubly chilling, that a woman who was physically compromised by layers of clothing in extreme heat could be physically assaulted for a minor act of self-protection. That her attacker was her son or sister-son, that he was a child, that his behavior aroused not the slightest reaction from the public or her spouse were all very disturbing. That boy, or his sons, are the Taliban now, raised on violence toward women, including their own mothers, as a way of life.

What could I do? Shout that this was immoral, unacceptable, wrong? Smack the child's arrogant face, an initial impulse? Rail at the father and the other men who accepted and allowed this abusive behavior? I didn't expect the woman to discipline the child, though I wished her culture would allow her to. I couldn't do any of the above without creating a major incident, but I could show kindness and support for the women. I made it my business to glare at the sullen child at every opportunity for the next several hours. By gesture, the women had been insistent on repairing Tony's ripped shirt, when the sewing was finally done, they presented it to him with a flourish. I had highly regarded sweets and treats from the Qandahar bazaar and indulged the women repeatedly, pressing expensive confections and drinks upon them over a period of hours. The now-petulant child was completely ignored. The father didn't merit a single glance. I think my deliberate rudeness made a slight impression on the father and child, a small and Pyrrhic victory.

We journeyed onward, ever closer to Kabul. My fellow American Bob was eagerly anticipating the culinary delights of this international city. Weeks of chewy nan and onions, supplemented by Fanta and occasional mystery mush, was stagnating to the palate. We hoped that our bouts of bacillic and amoebic dysentery were behind us, and the focus on our behinds was done too! The cuisine of Kabul was imminent. Bob's cup runneth over, he sat salivating in anticipation.

After checking in to a hotel, we took a taxi to a restaurant with the marvel of air conditioning. Thousands of miles of parching desert lay behind us; weeks and weeks of sweat runneling down our chests and dripping off our heads. Steaming nights and roasting days, drinking gross-tasting chlorine-treated water, enveloped in an ever-present aroma of sweat. To be standing in a fine restaurant with icy cold air blasting around us aroused such reverence, we nearly swooned. In the lobby, we inhaled the cooled air like formerly flopping fishes suddenly swimming in a deep delightful sea. The place had a dimly lit padded interior, a carpeted floor, and a limitless supply of orange juice at the bar. Everywhere were undulant waiters in white jackets with the requisite towels over their arms. We had traveled all night and were too eager to feast to wash the dust and reek of our journey away. We were weak, starving, and stinking, and I was embarrassed for the white glove service. The staff were perhaps more attuned to their tip than our offenses. Despite our begrimed and desert-worn appearance, we were westerners and in relative possession of the big bucks. We proceeded to indulge in a four-hour food fest, guzzling pitchers of cold juice while the kitchen readied our meal, Kabuli Chinese. Feasting on the delicious fare and the ambiance, my skin actually cooled to the point where it felt dry.

As cosmopolitan as Kabul was for that part of the world, it had the same pattern of morning ablutions as the rest of Afghanistan. The men would gather as the sun rose, squatting over the ever-present drainage ditches which made a gutter along every street. Conveniently, their cotton pants were split, with an opening along the seam in the crotch. My first morning in Afghanistan had been an oddly uncomfortable one until I realized why the men were staring a tad uneasily. Western sanitation practices were unknown. Every Afghan city and sizeable town had its drainage ditches, the water running through served as toilet and fountain both. Water was water in this world. Microbes and coliform counts had no place here. Unfortunately, I had seen too many kettles filled from those same ditches to be okay drinking anything that was not bottled. In Kabul, it was the same. There were more painted lorries, more citizens, more exhaust fumes, and more bazaars, but the daily rhythm was uniquely that of Afghanistan.

Perusing a copy of a Kurt Vonnegut paperback at a book seller's stall near the hotel, the ragged urchin who ran the stall suddenly piped up, "Yes, yes, very good Vonnegut book, Mrs.!" I don't know if I was more startled by his English or his appreciation of countercultural icons. Likely, he just knew a hot item when he saw one.

It was in Kabul that Malcolm, Tony, and Kevin made their departure for points east. They had many miles to go before they could lay their journey down. Bob and I were only going to India, they were going across Burma and Thailand to Oz and the land of the Māori. The parting had been difficult.

Malcolm was angry because I would not give up my India quest to go with him to Woolonga, his multimillion-acre sheep ranch in Australia. His gender bender tales of the Australian outback social scene, perhaps or perhaps not exaggerated in way of preparation, had held little appeal. In truth, I was not interested in settling anywhere with anyone at that time. Despite his blond handsomeness, stalwart strength, and other charms, I couldn't commit to going to his home with him. I was enjoying being the American beauty on the road. Tomorrow was down that road, and the price of the possibility was having to move on. It always is.

Tony was dear to me, a self-deprecating man full of humor and warmth. He good-naturedly endured our teasing and name-calling, based on raucous nights in a taverna on the Greek island of Thassos, where he had been invited by the owner to make the acquaintance of his best female donkey. Having spent a year in England exploring their roots in British culture, bfs Tony and Kevin were on their way back to the north island of New Zealand. Tony had a rollicking sense of humor and a dry British wit. I would miss the lightness and the laughter that were such a part of who he was.

Kevin was the one who got away. He had a sensitive soul and a soulful look in his blue eyes. His poetic nature and artistic temperament spoke loudly to me. In truth, it had been a four-alarm fire. This was a man I could fall in love with, and that was too dangerous. I undoubtedly hurt him by not choosing him, but I was still on the run from the double beds of the world. Letting him go meant the end of my dream that we would be together when I was ready. When Nelson Mandela went to prison, Winnie wrote "Part of My Soul Went with Him." [(9)] I grieved for what Kevin and I would never have.

Losing these friends, forever, left a big hole in the fabric of my life. It also left me with Pennsylvania Bob. I should have been far more compassionate. What a wicked first excursion outside of the familiar confines of the USA. He was a boy who had wanted to fly straight into India. Instead, he found himself traipsing across the badlands of the Middle East as a part of my entourage. If he complained from time to time because there was no lemonade, who was I to judge? Bob loved sweets, the mosquitoes ate him alive, the black flies favored his green eyes and fleas found him tasty as well. He carried an insulated jug on his hip, in remembrance of refrigeration, and a picture of his guru, who we were going to see. I had had a romance or two with interesting young men who followed this man. These were the days following the Beatles' sojourn to Rishikesh, which introduced the western world to meditation and triggered much wonder about the wisdom of the East. In the era of "Peace Now," long before the understanding of DNA, the East held an intriguing key to the mystery of life.

The bird market of Ka Farushi, a dim warren of winding alleys bustling with activity, was cooler than the outside streets and captivating for its richness of avian song. Nowhere in Afghanistan was modern dress seen, and this included the streets of Kabul. The women were fully covered in their black chadors, and the men dressed in traditional style according to their ethnicity. The most common dress was Pathan, a long loose shirt to the knees covering wrapped cotton trousers, a short waist coat, and turban. Almost every male had a full beard. There are photos of young women on the streets of Kabul from this era, showing leg in miniskirts and western dress. While I saw women dressed in western clothing in Teheran, I never saw it in Afghanistan.

The Afghans loved Americans, although the great cities of New York and LA or Chicago were unknown. Kabul was cosmopolitan enough that I could feel comfortable walking the few miles between a friend's hotel and mine. There were macrobiotic restaurants, friendly bazaars, book sellers of western paperbacks, and a large international community heading both east and west on the trail. At Sigi's, on Chicken Street, the freak flag was flying. The international set hung loose, sprawled on cushions in the garden. Marijuana and hashish perfumed the air. Afghanistan, the haven, the refuge, the best smoke in the world, embraced the flower children with open arms. California Bob blew into town on his Harley. We found each other again, but he was still hung up on the girl he left behind in L.A. It was one of those tales where the heart cleaves rigidly to an outmoded concept, at the cost of the potential of the present. I later heard she had found someone else almost before his flight landed in Europe.

The Pushtuns at Sigi's, forerunners of future Taliban, plied us with pillows and tea and curds and ran to the bazaars to purchase our every need. We spent afternoons in the garden, drinking chai, sniffing flowers, and nursing our delicate digestions. There was a live chessboard for our entertainment, with Pushtun warriors serving as rooks and knights. The game was played on a grassy square in the center of the lawn, with the warriors moving about the board, following the commands of the guests. They even took orders from women, laughing, and spelled each other standing on the squares or darting off the chessboard to eagerly tend to the needs of guests. Their service was so seamless, they seemed to undulate. Although music was frowned upon by the Prophet, at times it played softly for our pleasure. Catering to our total comfort and every wish was the MO. The more jaded among us thought it was all about money, but I sensed a dedication that went far deeper than coin.

It was at Sigi's that I spent an afternoon transfixed by a stunning English-speaking Pathan warrior. He proudly and respectfully told me of the Pushtunwali, the code of honor, which includes the rite of guest welcome. These men were embracing *melmestia*, the practice of showing hospitality and heartfelt respect for all visitors, and *pat*, the respect for all existences. *Melmestia* is practiced with no goal of remuneration or earthly reward and is considered a sacred honor to extend to all guests regardless of religion, race or country of origin. In honoring us, the warriors were serving their tribal identity and an ancient behavioral code established a millennium before the birth of Christ. The code of honor also mandates a fighting spirit, righteousness, and faith, sanctuary, loyalty, and bravery. The Pushtunwali requires respect for all peoples, all living creatures, and for the environment. Scholars interpret the code and its implications differently. While there is no doubt that justice, vengeance, and blood debt are included in the code, my experience as an outlander on the receiving end of *melmestia* and *pat* led me to believe that in the warmth of the welcome of the Pushtun, I had found the true heartlands of Islam.

Chapter

# 9

# Women's Gynecological Hospital, Kabul

The American Embassy in Kabul was an imposing glass and concrete structure, emblazoned with eagles on its doors. In deference to my trail mate Bob, we were applying for visas for both Pakistan and India, as he did not wish to linger any longer on the road. Processing took an hour or two, I wandered the spacious white corridors cooled by whirring ceiling fans and dotted with potted palms. The moving air and calm efficiency were in soothing contrast to the teeming streets outside of the compound. Surprisingly, there were few Americans, the busy staff seemed to be all Afghans, hundreds of workers engaged in the activities of the American consulate. They worked in large rooms, quietly conferring and taking notes, efficiently performing with no sense of urgency or stress. The toilets were clean squatters but struck a discordant note as five-inch cockroaches emerged from them.

Holed up in Kabul, waiting for the cooling monsoon to hit India, I felt seriously vulnerable for the first time. Mail from the post restante had brought on a wave of homesickness. My mother's chatty letter from New York was a month old. My Deutsch friend Christian wrote from Hamburg, a pretty city of geranium-decked balconies, reconstructed after the bombings of World War II. He unexpectedly declared his love for me, sending my head spinning in new directions. I was on the road with only one young man who was clearly uncomfortable, and out of his depth. Our health was in decline, both of us suffering from a recurrence of boiling bowel syndrome, likely another dysentery. Our hotel recommended a doctor who lived nearby. His children's Fisher Price toys littered the alleyway behind the hotel, a familiar sight. The doctor was British–trained, fluent in English, the real deal. After the last medic in Herat, who had pressed his body against mine at every opportunity, I felt enormously reassured.

The doc came to our hotel room for blood and stool samples. Bob and I were the only two left of the original cast of characters, Steve the Brit had departed for India as well. We were simply too ill to move on. Bob had a cold on top of his bowel troubles, his bed was littered with the dirty tissues of his misery. Fearful of hepatitis, I watched to be certain that the doctor used a fresh needle for the blood draw. He set me up with rubber tubing, broke open the needle's new packaging, and before my very eyes, used a snotty tissue to wipe inside my elbow and jabbed the needle home.

There was much worse to come. The tests showed that I had amoebic dysentery, and the doc felt the need for a gynecological exam. He drove Bob and I to the Kabul Women's Gynecological Hospital in his sedan. The rooms were full of new mothers and squalling babies. Veil less, when the women saw the doctor in the hallway, they instantly drew covering over their faces, putting it off again as soon as he passed by. I wondered exactly how delivery was accomplished here. Were faces covered while working parts were exposed? Or was this doctor a stranger to the women, necessitating the veiling? Their eyes were fixed solely on him, our presence seemed incidental. Was it that all infants born under the chador, and only those with penises allowed out?

The examination room had a red leatherette table and stirrups. I was not prepared for such stark and antiquated equipment. It looked like Doctor Frankenstein's laboratory. The kindly doctor's demeanor changed completely. He refused to enter the room with me, bringing in three women, who gestured to me to assume the position.

The worst moment of any gynecological exam is not being flat on your back with your legs wide open. It's not the stirrups or the cold metal speculum or even the pinch when your cervix is scraped. It's the moment when the doctor shines the lamp between your spread legs and looks up into your eyes, saying you are too far away. You must slide your exposed and glistening genitalia ever closer to his face. This exam was no exception, and as I began the slide, I heard a sudden snort in the vicinity of my nether regions. A natural strawberry blonde, my light pubic hair was a source of amazement in this world. The chortling female assistants poked each other in the ribs, called in their friends, elbowed one another for the best view, all the while jabbering, guffawing and laughing derisively out loud. There must have been twenty of them, and the doctor was rattled. He finished the exam and bailed, suddenly yanking the door open to escape the room. A man was sprawled upside down on his head looking under the door. It seems that he had heard the commotion and had to have a look. He was on hands and knees, peering in with his head upside down under the door jamb, when the door was jerked open and he fell on his face. The women screamed, the doctor ran, my crotch was the sensation of Afghanistan.

Chapter

# 10

# DEATH ROOSTS IN THE KHYBER

The witches in Jalalabad called loudly to one another. Alors! Alors! They wore sackcloth, were barefoot, and had significant facial disfigurement. The older sister had huge quivering growths which hung off the end of her nose. The younger one had lesions that looked likely to blossom into full-fledged nodules. I thought perhaps they were lepers.

I had seen them on the trail in other countries, always dressed in white sacks, always barefoot. They carried French passports and very little else. This time, as we climbed into the truck that would take us through the Khyber Pass, the older one was smiling. She was with a local man who was obviously undeterred by her facial anomalies. Perhaps she made great love talk in French.

Perhaps she put a bag over her head. They had no English, and my French was not adequate to their complexities.

Tourist information described Jalalabad as a resort destination with a pleasant climate. Was there more than one Jalalabad? I liked its older name, Gandhara, the city that overlooked two valleys. The Moghul emperor Babur had founded it in the 1500's. The British held it against Afghan siege many times, and died 16,000 men, women, and children trying to get through the mountains back to India.

We climbed aboard a green metal truck with a roof over its bed and twelve hard metal seats. Les soeur Française sat in front of me. The driver was armed with a shotgun. It was the guard who was arresting, however. A tall Pushtun, he wore ammunition belts crossed upon his chest like Pancho Villa. He had a dozen rifles and boxes of ammunition and extra-long-barreled weapons stacked up on the floor. The word was that the passage through the Khyber was the most dangerous part of the journey overland to India. Bandits would sweep down from the cliffs, shoot all the men in the head, and carry off the women. As the only women on board were me and the unsightly sisters, I knew I was prime meat.

I must admit the scenario had a certain romantic appeal. A warrior on horseback racing down from the heights and pulling me into the saddle, pulses pounding. He should ride like the wind, with a strong muscular body, sinews cloaked in the lion's skin......more likely, he would be a mad, malodorous miscreant with a dread bolt and a penchant for violence. Away, moldy rogue, away! [10]

Pennsylvania Bob, my lone traveling companion, was not exactly Indiana Jones material. I had high hopes for the armed guard, though. In Kabul, there were posters of Pushtun warriors bristling with weapons plastered all over the streets. They blazed with heat and ammunition and wore fierce expressions to match their awesome machismo. I had laughed at the time, marveling at cultural differences and how seriously they took themselves. Humor was harder to find out here.

The drive through the Khyber was stifling. The sun beat down on the metal vehicle, turning it into an oven. We were stopped before the pass, delayed for an unknown reason. The heat was fierce, far hotter than the day before, which had topped 112. I calculated it to be around 120 degrees. Sweat dripped off the back of my head onto my neck. It runneled between my breasts, ran down my face, but the incessant drip, drip, drip onto my neck was making me crazy. Mindful of dehydration, I drank the chlorine-treated tinny water and the taste of it sickened me. I also sweated running out of water before we got through the pass. I had visions of the Lewis and Clarke expedition, broken axles and hostile natives swooping out of nowhere. I thought of my hero, Sir Richard Burton, upstream on the Congo River in a hollowed-out log. A thousand miles from nowhere, with little prospect of return, he asked himself "why" and answered "the devil drives." [11] My devils still had me on the run from the double beds of the world.

We were still stuck out in the sun, broiling bandit bait under the metal roof of the truck. Insane people of at least five nationalities were on board this contraption parching in the noonday heat. This place made Death Valley seem a walk in the park. The locals said "Death roosts in the Khyber and preens its wings."[12] I said "Inshallah, I will survive this."

The younger French sister had dysentery. She vomited quietly and endlessly out of her window. Sitting behind her, in an agony of heat prostration, I must admit that the slight mist of her vomit spraying back through the window was delightfully cooling. It had come to that. The heavily armed guard walked purposefully back toward the vomiting girl. "KEEP YOUR HEAD DOWN!" he commanded, not in English or French, but his meaning was clear. He gestured to her to vomit onto the floor. Then he pointed up to the cliff tops with his rifle and I thought I saw movement. I slunk down low on the hard metal seats.

The Khyber Pass was moonscape. There was no color, no relief from the endless monochromatic xeriscape, just rocks and featureless waste. Not a single blade of grass could be seen, not one plant, not one tree. The word "Khyber" derives from the Hebrew, and means fort. This thirty-mile-long fortress pass connects the Northwest Frontier Territory of Pakistan with Afghanistan, in the heart of Pushtun country. It is walled on the north side by steep, unclimbable rocky cliffs, which rise vertically from the valley floor an angle of nearly 180 degrees. Those unforgiving crags made me aware that I was entering Everest and K2 territory. I was in the shadow of the earth's mightiest mountain deities, man-killers. Through these dangerous defiles had passed the camel caravans of antiquity, and had marched the great armies of the Greeks, Aryans, Persians, Scythians, Huns, Mongols, and Tartars. And in my day and time, thousands of flower children were just passin' through.

The old caravan route still existed, but the British had built a road through in the 1870's. They also put in a railroad line in the 1920's, costing more than two million pounds. Two million 1920's British pounds, equivalent to many more millions today. The railroad lasted about fifty years. Its route featured 34 tunnels, 92 bridges, a 425-foot drop in 7/10ths of a mile, and likely cardiac arrest. It was my only other option then, the only alternative to broiling as bandit bait.

The walls of the Khyber curved, carved by floods in eons past. A mile wide at maximum, its width was 16 yards when narrowing in, ambush made easy. There was an arresting man-made feature, however. Thousands upon thousands of prayer flags, rags tied to poles stuck into the crumbling rock, stirring not. Not a breath of wind was present to cause the slightest motion. The effect was completely eerie. I surmised they were grave markers, and thought of the hundreds of thousands of souls who had lost their lives in this bleak terrain. When the pass waxed wide, it offered a vantage of the surrounding monochromatic scree and the formidable Hindu Kush. In the narrower spots the tension mounted, all of us scanning the pressing heights with total vigilance, fearful of the slightest hint of raiders on horseback. I saw motion several times, several times our guard squared his shoulders, checked his ready status and pointed his weapons. I hung onto the conversations of the guard and the driver, in Pushtu, listening for the alarm in their voices that would announce the end of my world as I knew it. It never came. We were through.

Chapter

# 11

☷

# PASSING THROUGH PAKISTAN

Peshawar, the final frontier, 1975, on the wrong side of town. As capitol of the Northwest Frontier province, it was a place of pandemonium and bedlam; a chaotic, decrepit, hellacious, slum-ridden, bandit-infested, decaying wooden city. The din, the press of wild men, the atmosphere of absolute lawlessness unnerved and alarmed. Every man was packing, most with several weapons in evidence. Some had two six shooters in gun belts on their hips, like Wyatt Earp. There were Smith and Wessons and Colts and Derringers dangling from breast pockets like handkerchiefs would be. These dudes would bust a cap as soon as look at you, or better yet just shoot your legs out beneath you.

Women were very scarce. The sister wives under the chadors were gone. Family life evidently did not exist in this part of town. I saw no open-air bazaars, no jewelry sellers, no one interested in anything but covert action. It was guns and slums and crows of characters garbed straight out of the Old Testament. Ethnic lines were easily blurred. While Pakistan was formed from the western part of India to create an Islamic homeland, the region has borne many invasions and belonged to many empires. The Indus River and its five tributaries flow between the Arabian Sea to the south and India's Punjab plain to the east. Pakistan's richly watered valleys and agricultural lands have drawn the eye of conquerors further back than recorded history. Early humans, migrating out of Africa, first settled this region. A high Buddhist culture flourished in the area near Gandhara and elsewhere in what is now known as Pakistan. There are abundant artifacts and coins to be found, Baluchistan Province alone is literally strewn with the remains of earlier civilizations. The Indus Valley Buddhist culture gave way to the Aryans before the Persian Empire held the region, with the famed general Darius in the lead. The Pax Persica allowed for allowed for the local rulers to swear token fealty to him and establish a flourishing economy. Darius, the Persian conqueror, wrested territories away from the Greeks all the way to the Danube River in Europe. This aroused the ire of the Greek general known as Alexander the Great, who came gunning for Pakistan determined to kick butt because of Greece's humiliation by Darius. He annexed the country and the nearby Punjab, but his unexpected demise led to rulership by the Punjabi Mauryans, who eventually converted to Buddhism. The first circle was complete. The Greeks eventually returned, the fierce

Huns then ruled for 600 years, and Islamic rule began in 1227. Battles with the Sikhs, lords of the Punjab, carried forward the instability of the region until the British partitioned India, creating the Islamic Republic of Pakistan in 1947. The partition cleaved the tribal Pushtun lands in two, inflaming the hostilities that persist to this day.

The Pushtun presence in Pakistan, was even larger than in Afghanistan. Some scholars consider the Pathans to be the descendants of the lost tribes of Israel. Certainly, many of their custom speak of Hebrew heritage. Newborn males are circumcised on the eighth day instead of the twelfth year. Pushtun names translate to Ephraim and Asher, names of the lost tribes. The legal system and code of ethics, the Pushtunwali, is akin to the Torah, and even names Moses. The facial features, elongated shapes and beards, the fairer skin and light eyes shared by both Pushtun and Jew all point to a common ancestry. This would be easy to ascertain now via DNA testing, but to my knowledge, this has not been explored. Most convincing was the sight of the Star of David commonly seen over the doorways of Pushtun homes and their public schools. There are old stories of Pushtun elders appearing at synagogues in prayer shawls on the high holy days. This theory does put the Pushtun issue and the conflicts of the Middle East in a different light. If the actual ancestors of the Taliban were the Jews, then one must consider that the descendants of the lost tribes became declared enemies of Israel.

In 1975, the descendants of all of the above were a seething mix on the streets of Peshawar, heavily armed and dangerous. Some say the name Peshawar derives from the Sanskrit and means "City of Flowers." Others claim the name translates from the Mughal, meaning "City at the Frontier." For us, all plans of finding a hotel to for the night were off. We wanted to be on the first stagecoach out of town, preferably before sundown. I was sorry to miss the Fort and the Kissa Khavani bazaar, home of storytellers and songbirds and multilingual live theatre. It was sad to be unable to visit the Gurakabrastan graveyard, where the thousands lie after their slaughter in the Khyber Pass. Considered to be actively haunted, the place was untended and decaying even then, but I had wanted to feel the echoes and pay homage to the lost ancestral gene pool. Peshawar was and is known for its superabundance of professional thieves. The melting pot drew renegades and outlaws of many nationalities because of the chaos, lawlessness, and corruption. I felt like I had time-warped into an alien version of the Old West. Years later, watching Star Wars and Chewbacca in the intergalactic saloon scene, I had a strong déjà vu. Chewy was fighting off increasingly bizarre life forms, I knew this scene! Peshawar! [13]

We shot across the northwest of Pakistan, heading east and south in a nightmare of ramshackle slums, teeming multitudes and disease in the cities along the Peshawar Road. We had no one to advise us or suggest a better route. Rawalpindi was among the many stops, not finding the rail line, a bus ticket was our only way out. This was public transportation, the lowest class, charter buses and tourist amenities a dream. Beggars began to appear in earnest, and they were no longer easy-going and sound of body. With missing hands, arms, or feet, covered with oozing sores and crusts, they were angry about their lot in life, and rightfully so. Blind men stalked the roads. The whites of their eyes were overgrown and covered by a reddened network of blood vessels, their pupils and irises gone. Some were led and others walked heavily, leaning on staffs. The overgrown white membranes were shockingly laced with vivid red blood vessels. There were so many sightless. I thought of schistosomiasis or other water-borne parasites as the cause of this science fiction parade. The five rivers of the Indus seemed to have devil spawn. Malarial mosquitoes whined, I downed my quinine doses faithfully, with thanks. Lepers wandered, bumps and rotting rags. My amoebic dysentery and Bob's bacillic problem were fortunately blasts from the past. Our view of Pakistan was undoubtedly very jaded by our travels from the hovel bus depot of Peshawar to its peers in Rawalpindi and Lahore. We missed the K2 and the towering peaks of the Kara Korum and the Hindu Kush. The coniferous forests on their slopes held snow leopards, bear, wolf, and otter. The crocodiles of the Indus flood plains were MIA too, and the gazelles and peacocks of the Thor Desert. The legendary Hunza Valley, home to one of the longest-lived populations on earth, remained shrouded in inaccessible mystery. The Peshawar Road and most of the Pakistani population were jammed into the usable one third of the country. The remote and romantic northernmost region, home of the Kaffirs, the reclusive descendants of Alexander's armies, would have to wait for another lifetime.

There is another story of Pakistan, engraved upon my memory, that the mercies of time have diminished but not taken away. I have known men who have been jailed, their recollected horror of the prison door slamming reverberates inside them for always. So too did I recoil when the door slammed, and I was caged. My crime? Being female of the species with vulva and a womb. One late night in darkness, dulled with fatigue after being on the road so long the sun had risen and set and risen and set again, I climbed onto a public bus behind my companion, Bob. It was in a rural area, hours outside of any city, heading east in pursuit of the border with India. The driver snarled at me, yelling and making threatening motions to kick me. I thought there was a problem with the tickets, but the hostility was too great. Bob sat down, distressed, gently directing my attention to the back of the bus. Amidst the angry barrage of words from the driver, I turned my head. The last third of the bus was a cage. Steel bars separated the males from the females. I admit I panicked as I was pushed down the stairs and separated from Bob, my only tie to the familiar. If I were left on this dark road in the middle of the night alone, it could mean my death. Or worse. I thought I was seeing the last of the familiar, the last moment of everything that I knew, left alone in a cloud of diesel on a dingy street on a god forsaken night on the other side of the world. Women were stoned to death here. Trembling, I heard Bob's voice above the din, telling me to get to the door at the back of the bus. I fully expected the driver, his face contorted by his outrage, to leave me in the road. Sprinting for the door, heavily unbalanced in in my backpack, I got my foot on the first stair before the driver gunned the engine, and fell inside.

Welcome to Purdah, and the back of the bus. While some of the intent might have been protective, the reality to an American felt like being jailed for being female. I found a seat, still shaking. I looked to the veiled woman sitting nearby for support. She back looked back at me with contempt, and deliberately turned her gaze away. I was so stunned by the experience that I stared, still seeking some empathy from her, but she deliberately pulled her voluminous black veils ever closer to her body with her black-gloved hands. My apparent violation of norms was more egregious to her than any sense of gender solidarity or compassion that I might be seeking. More women joined us at the next stop and then a man appeared with a big metal key and locked us all inside. The women were clearly offended at my presence, and studiously ignored my glances at them. I stood by the bars of the cage, anxiously chattering with Bob, which further engendered hostilities. Apparently a woman was supposed to sit down and shut up, her eyes lowered so as not to offend by the temerity of her glances. As I continued to talk to Bob, the only object of familiarity in this ordeal, I could feel a tide of antagonism rising. A few of the women were looking at me now, anger in their body language. Would they hit me? Pull my hair? Worse? So I took a seat on a hard wooden bench under a window, surrounded by the utter blackness of the Pakistani night. There were no street lights or any signs of electricity. I thought ironically of Michael Rockefeller, eaten by cannibals at twenty-three. I thought of Rosa Parks, who paid her fare at the front of the bus, but had to find a seat through the rear door. The endless night rolled on, with infrequent shadows slinking in the inky dark, and stumbling women exiting into the night. I contemplated man's inhumanity, to man, and women's in humanity to women.

Chapter

# 12

☰

# THE RAJ TOTTERS ON

The Indian border was closed and shuttered to the night. I was exhausted, impatient, strung out, but there was no recourse but to wait by the border station, dozing in the dark. One eye or was ear always open, expecting hostilities. The oppressive disdain accorded to a stranger in a strange land had worn me down. The relentlessness of my differences— American, single, female, tall and blonde, light eyed, who could never fit in or hide out under a veil....it had all accumulated and taken its toll. There was no respite, no privacy, no sense of security, and for the last forty-eight hours, no sleep. I maintained a state of semi consciousness, uneasy.

Glimmers in the pearly gray dawn gradually appeared. I awoke on the Indian border surrounded by the lush ladies of the sari. They lay on chaise lounges luxuriating in their silk garments with rolls of belly fat proudly on display. Only the very rich could afford to buy and store sustenance as flesh. These regal women, secure in their sense of entitlement, gave sharp orders to the male waiters who suddenly appeared with tea trays, clapping their hands to hurry the obsequious fellows along. Hands, arms, necks, and faces were uncovered and exposed, along with the belly rolls and soft hennaed feet. Their saris were a riot of bright colors; blues and pinks and yellows, and the air around them wafted fragrant with sandalwood. I was utterly astonished. Gone were the women who covered every square inch of their flesh in black drapes and veils.

The dawn held other delights. Parrots flitted in the shrubs, brightly colored singing birds of reds and greens and impossible turquoises. Every hue was super saturated. The restaurant which had spawned the waiters proved to be a relaxing place where women could sit alone, unremarked. I ordered my first lassi on the Indian border, a fruit and yoghurt drink flavored with rosewater. As the rich and sensual flavors exploded in my mouth, I knew it as a milestone. A boundary had been crossed between what had been and what would be. The contrast drenched my senses.

My intriguing new reality was not yet attained. The border guards decided I might be smuggling rupees, which I was, unaware that carrying the currency across the border was illegal. For the equivalent of about fifty U.S. dollars, I was subjected to a startlingly intrusive strip search and a lot of verbal hammering. Again and again my rupee stash was demanded. The female guard belittled me in her own language. When I told her that rupees could be freely purchased in New York, she thought I was a liar, the concept too outlandish for a border guard in Amritsar. I cried foul, loudly ranting "set up;" that the Indian government was selling American citizens rupees in the U.S. and then abusing those citizens when they tried to cross the border with them. At that time, holding a passport from the great U.S. democracy that epitomized what the rest of the world yearned for had considerable clout. My accusations on the abuse of my civil rights proved persuasive and gained my release.

At the British-built train station, coolies scuttled about, moving mountains of passengers' luggage. I tried to carry my own, creating a commotion and causing the chief porter to cry out in protest. He indignantly pointed to the metal badge he wore pinned to his chest which was stamped "Coolie #10." The term I considered to be an ethnic slur was actually a source of pride to this man. I was insulting him and diminishing his rightful earnings by my well-meaning actions contrary to custom. Handing over my luggage for storage in the baggage room, I headed off to find the ladies' parlor for tea. Remnants of the Raj tottered on. On an upholstered chair amidst potted ferns, my feet resting on an ottoman, the ceiling fan whirring a teak-scented breeze, I read a London newspaper and happily mulled my escape. No one does civility better than the Brits.

Amritsar was the capitol of the plains state of Punjab. It was the spiritual and agricultural home of the Sikhs and the site of their Golden Temple. The Sikhs were culturally separate from the rest of India, with a unique religion, mode of dress, social system, and roles for women in society. With their beliefs in reincarnation, karma, and the sacredness of animal life, the Hindu derivation is obvious. The distinctions are many, however. The founder of Sikhism attacked the Hindu caste system, and supported women's rights and full participation in society. As early as 1499, the leader launched a campaign to increase respect and appreciation for women. The supreme deity in Sikhism is considered to be genderless, not male. Women have the right to vote on religious matters, read scripture, and foster their spirituality, as the female soul is considered to be equal to the male. In the 1600's, the Sikh leader abolished the veiling of women and the horrendous custom of sati, the burning of wives on the funeral pyre of a recently deceased male. "From woman, kings are born; from woman, woman is born; without woman, there would be no one at all. So why call her bad?"[14] Widely acknowledged for their industry, organization, and executive skills, Sikhs have endured much discrimination within Hindu society. A Hindu told me that a Sikh must always wear a sword and underwear, the former to battle Muslims as the need arises and the latter to never be caught with their pants down! In reality, the underwear symbolizes control of the passions and the bangle on the right wrist reminds the wearer that no evil shall be done by his hand. The swords were symbolic label pins, even then. Impressive ideology, perhaps not fully realized in a nation where unwanted wives are still disposed of by gasoline.

Sikhs are prohibited from cutting their hair, traditionally observing men wear a topknot and full beard. Women often never cut their hair. In public, a man's top knot is covered by a turban. The ignorant are not able to distinguish between a Sikh and a Muslim, hurling the ethnic slur "raghead" at both. In fact, there is a strong history of enmity and conflict between Sikh and Muslim, beginning with the Battle of Amritsar in 1634. The geographical overlap between the Mughal empires and the Sikh tenancy of the plain of the Punjab has served as fuel, along with other factors. The Taliban have levied financial penalties upon Sikhs in Pakistan in recent times. The unenlightened in the west subject both groups as one to hate crimes, bullying, and profiling.

The train ride across the Punjab was rich in agricultural sights but the relentless heat soon overwhelmed. The temperatures exceeded 100 F. Teeming railway stations offered little round dishes of the unknown upon trays, rather like dim sum, but I mostly declined. This was handmade food ladled out and carried by humans who did not necessarily value the connection between dirt and illness. I did accept tea, however, glorious steaming brew of unimagined flavor and intensity. One never expects the wealth of tastes of India's teas. Although cultivation was not introduced until the

1830's, its service was quickly institutionalized by the Brits. The cash revenues earned a place in the national economy, a familiar tale of profits owned by foreign corporations and exploitation of indigenous laborers. Tea leaves must be hand-picked, at various stages of color, shape, and curl. Smaller female hands are considered to be more suitable to this work, and conditions in the major tea-growing regions of India remained feudalistic and exploitative in modern times.

Innocent of these policies, my friends and I often took tea at the legendary Wenger House in New Delhi. We explored the pleasures of Assam and Darjeeling blends amidst the rich mahogany panels and sterling silver tea services at this bastion of British propriety. There was no air conditioning, but the well-oiled ceiling fans circulated cooling breezes, and the elegance of the wooden appointments furnished us with a rich sense of ease. After a few languorous visits, soaking in the ambiance of luxury, the sight of the petit fours served to rouse me. The self-indulgent torpor in which I was indulging may have been a natural consequence of weeks of deprivation. The petit fours were over the top though, sweet little cakes of pristine whiteness, iced in chocolate and adorned with swirls and squiggles of perfect pink. There were lepers and legless beggars right outside the door. Their families could live for a month for the price of one dainty little cake.

We stayed in Old Delhi, teeming with masses of
fine-featured, dark-skinned poor. This was partly to not
support elitist tourism, partly because we were tough
enough, and happily because our friends Malcolm, Kevin,
and Tony had materialized out of thin air. Kevin was still
mystical, and Malcolm was still blond. Delighting in being
together again unexpectedly, we healed old wounds and
forged new bonds of affection. We were all lower key than
we had been in Afghanistan, the continuity of culture
from Istanbul to the Khyber Pass was now history.
Finding ourselves in unfamiliar territory, we needed to get
our bearings, learn the rules, suss out the situation. Many
westerners stayed holed up in their hotel rooms, unable to
cope with the noise, the beggars, the heat, the humidity,
the smells, the press of humanity, the garbage, the flies,
the cows.

New Delhi was Carnivale on acid. Every road the
British built was a roundabout; one taxied around in
endless circles with no escape, horns honking and exhaust
fumes billowing. Most striking were the motorcycle
mamas on their Vespas. Women did not have their own
scooters, of course, that would have been too permissive
for this patriarchal society. But those sisters rode
sidesaddle on their men's machines with great aplomb.
Their multicolored saris and gorgeous scents fluttered on
the wind. Horns honked by the thousands, motors revved,
vehicles careened madly. The fragrant women perched,
regal amidst the chaos, handspun silk blouses under their
saris, adorned in bangle bracelets, foreheads painted in

reds and ochers, with jeweled hennaed feet. Black braids hung to their knees. They were dark-eyed butterflies in the wind on the wings of Vespa, unforgettable. The women were too refined to be wild, although the scene was. There was a sense of propriety and formality to upper class Indian women. Duty to family was paramount, filial piety the norm, marriages were still arranged. Yet there were places on this large subcontinent where women drank herbs giving "stamina for the night of a thousand husbands" and were taught to bring men to orgasm by the rhythmic clenching of their vaginal walls.

Delhi abounded with sights and sites. The Red Fort, all looming red sandstone, was crowded with snake charmers and sadhus. The snakes, opiated and fangless, rose on cue out of their baskets, swaying sinuously to the reed music. Many of the wandering sadhus were aggressive fortune tellers who often spoke English. Malcolm returned from a sadhu encounter at the Red Fort in shock, having been recited private details of his relationship with his deceased mother that defied rational explanation. He could not fathom it and sat with his head in his hands and his eyes cast down, his world rocked. I rushed off to the Red Fort eagerly. The wild man who approached me was intimidating, tall and emaciated, decked out in a well-worn loincloth. He came right into my face, arms windmilling, yelling that there were two men who loved me (Indians disapprove of multiple interests) and that I would leave India very soon. I had just arrived, just survived a rigorous overland journey of thousands of miles. My plan was to spend six months in country, journey up to Nepal, and then go on to Tibet if a visa came through. These undesired predictions earned him no coin from me.

The streets were a cacophony. Gaunt and giant brahma bulls wandered down roads covered with refuse and excrement. Humans swarmed, clothing sweat-plastered to their skins, nonchalant in the blistering heat. Billowing flies clustered so that one could not see more than forty feet ahead, sight lines obscured by thick and buzzing clouds of insects. Fruit stands abounded, blenders whirring, whizzing up papaya and mango smoothies, cooling concoctions of utter deliciousness. Fruit peels were at times calf-deep, attracting animals who foraged, dogs and pigs and huge bulls. I was fascinated by their bone structure, sharply angled scapulae sticking hard up through their skins. The span of their horns was wider than my shoulders, their shoulders loomed well above my own. They were invisible to the people of Delhi, symbolic of sacred beings, convenient to lean on when one needed a break from navigating the vagaries of foot traffic. Little automobiles gave the cows courteous right of way while pickle men hawked cold cucumbers on wheeled wagons in the streets. One day a bull nipped me on the shoulder, the bite of the bovine both unexpected and very sharp. It soon became easier to make forays only at night, when the human traffic had abated, and the beasts were in less profusion. The beggars, however, never went away.

Visiting the market one day early in my Delhi visit, an armless beggar got way too close. He was hostile of both expression and intent, corralling me as I turned a tight corner in a market stall and flapping his arms stumps in my face. They were jiggling caplets of flesh, cut off just where the deltoid muscles would insert below the shoulder joints. I only screamed the first time. It was said that the teeming poor of India had to maim their third-born and subsequent children because the family could not support them. Begging might. Eyes were cast out, and arms cut off. Feet were commonly amputated, or rotated 180 degrees at birth, so that the toes pointed backwards and the heels were in front. A cruel practice, which, being bloodless, saved lives. Homeless were everywhere, Untouchables, roasting ears of corn over little braziers on the streets. Some were angry, some were pathetic, and all were deeply disturbing. I was followed for city blocks by legless men who swung their torsos on their hands at amazing speeds, all the while whispering "Please, Memsahib, please." It was wrenching. I had the power to change their lives. I wanted to give to all the wretched humans who smiled and pleaded with their eyes. The more one gave, the more beggars laid in wait at the hotel door, surrounding and hounding. It became self-preservation to pretend they were unseen. I still saw.

Again we were stricken, this time with salmonella from the prawns and egg breakfasts at the morning markets. I shared a room with four men, we shared a bathroom down the hall with many others. A euphemism, really, it was just a squatter on the floor. There was no running water, the clay jars of the Middle East had given way to brass pitchers, we were still pouring with our right, and wiping with our left hands. There was a cloth hand towel on a continuous roller, mottled with brown and gray stains, awash, perhaps, in leprous tubercles. We all wore white cotton pants, drawstring knotted at the waist. Those knots proved troublesome, our bowels had turned to water, clear as H20 from a tap. Days of diarrhea weakened us all, snappish irritability and fatigue characterized too many interactions. Pharmaceuticals were precious now. Meeting with other westerners from Norway to South Africa, English was the universal language, sharing drugs the norm. Penicillin, sulfonamides, Lomotil, charcoal tablets, all exchanged as gestures of international good will. There was a serious hard drug scene too, hippies on their way to Goa to live on the beach and pick fruit off the trees, high on heroin. Wild boars lived there too, evolving with the freak population. The "shit-eating pigs of Goa" were legendary, tumbling hapless hippies in the sand, frenzied in their fights for feces. The boars were as big as golden retrievers, long of hair and mean of tusk. Bodily injury was the price of a junkie's dream.

It was time for Kevin and Tony to move onward towards New Zealand. Malcolm still wanted to take me to his ranch in Western Australia, but Australia was a long way from New York. I would have to commit to circling the globe, crossing the Pacific to get home. From India or Tibet, western civilization was a just dozen air hours west.

I had friends to return to in Denmark and Germany, sagas to continue. Bob and I went north, Kevin, Tony and Malcolm went east. I never saw them again.

Chapter

# 13

# SHAHJAHANPUR, UTTAR PRADESH

The train rolled through the northern Indian countryside. We had been warned of bandits, told to avoid cars in the rear of the train, which were most often ambushed. The breathless warnings might suitably intimidate those fresh from the lands of flush toilets and automatic doors. As veterans of the Silk Route and the Peshawar Road, we couldn't get it up for train robbers.

The spare first –class rail compartment reminded me of a jail cell, metal bars covering the window. To my surprise, raising the window raised the bars as well. Timeless India was outside. Ragged children drove herds of oxen under a steaming sky, tributaries of the Ganges flowed by, water buffalo meandered on the horizon. I stood by the window to drink the scene in. Sometimes a child drew close enough to see my face, and I watched the shock and incredulity register at the first sight of a fair-skinned human. I could have been from Mars. Reactions differed. Some ran like they had seen their worst nightmare. Many tried to keep up with the slow-moving train, calling excitedly to others to come and view the apparition. Some frowned and hurled stones at the window to drive off the evil spirit. Once I got a return smile, full of wonder. I had always dreamed the anthropological dream of being the first outsider seen by an indigenous people, a symbol of the far-off unknown. My aspiration was again realized that day, though I was glad of the framework of the railway car around me. There was more fear and intolerance in reality than my naïve expectations had prepared me for.

Children at the railway stations were unfazed by my strangeness. The stops were crowded and clamorous, with throngs of staring poor pressed up against the train windows, hands out in supplication. We ate little and slept as much as possible on our Spartan cushions. I had wanted a second- or third-class ticket to interact with the people, as any budding anthropologist would, but my companion wanted anything but. Our first-class tickets paid for privacy, not luxury.

After a twelve-hour train journey, we had our first glimpse of Shahjahanpur, teeming by torchlight. We hired a driver to carry us to the address of the compound of the Raja Yoga master whom we were to visit. The driver, a sturdy-legged little man, sat us on a shelf in his rickshaw, piled our luggage behind us and grabbed the handles of the cart. Onward. He proceeded to trot for miles and miles, barefoot, in the pitch darkness. The night was lit only by starlight and occasional oiled rag torches in the distance. Having no idea at all of where he was taking us, we could only hope that he was not leading us to our doom. Hills began to slow him; these were the foothills of the Himalayas. We walked beside the rickshaw, rather like a wheelbarrow with elongated wooden handles. The rickshaw runner wanted very much to know from whence we came, but the words "New York" and "Philadelphia" brought no recognition. Before he brought us to the gates of our destination, he got down on his knees, eyes filling with tears. Despite the language barrier, the intent was obvious. It was clear that he was imploring to be taken with us. The immensity of what we represented to this man was humbling.

It was nearly midnight when we arrived. We were a month early, just after the first rain of the season, not the end of the monsoon season. Oops. Accommodation in the westerners' dormitory were provided somewhat grudgingly as we had disturbed the compound with our late arrival. I didn't know what to expect from a Hindu holy man. Would he be a contemplative, serene, meditative type? I knew that he spoke English and six other languages, had been a householder and raised a family, and had been chosen by his predecessor to carry on a long lineage of the teachings of a type of Raja Yoga called Sahaj Marg. He was renowned for his abilities to speak an archaic poetic language consisting of couplets, mastered by very few. I thought perhaps he would instruct us in a fashion like a Zen master. Then again, he might be a kindly patriarch, a Holy Father like the Emperor of the Tarot, or gather his flock to him like the Hierophant of the Christians. Perhaps, just perhaps, he held the answers to the questions of the meaning of life.

Our first audience consisted of being led into his presence while he berated a servant. He railed at the hapless one, turned to us with no greeting, and promptly sat down to his hookah. It was a giant apparatus, four feet tall, and he perched silently on a chair to observe us, all the while burbling on his pipe. It was unnerving. Another servant displeased him, and he jumped up, standing silhouetted to the sun. I was mortified. He wore a dhoti, a thin white cotton wrap, and the sun shining through it illuminated his pendant testicles. His balls hung down halfway to his knees. Words failed me. Why was this happening? Where was the Prince of Peace?

Our second audience, that evening, consisted of being grilled by two elderly gentlemen regarding our purpose and expectations. One of them was friendly and inquisitive, with a lively manner. It was told that his son managed many affairs for the master and was clearly in his confidence. There was close scrutiny throughout the proceedings, minute observation by men who missed no detail.

We were fed alone, in a special open air dining area just for westerners. There was a roof and walls, but open space where doors and windows would have been. This allowed close up views of serving women, on their knees tending to huge clay pots which simmered over open fires. Flies by the hundreds of thousands covered every non-moving surface. Buzzing clouds of insects formed dark masses in the air. There was no electricity or running water, but a pump sat in the kitchen courtyard as the water source. A dour man came by and pointedly informed us that great pains had been taken to provide us with white bread and white rice. At the time, I was trying to politely extract dead flies from the curry. Cooked, they resembled peppercorns and other spices, but if one looked closely their sticky feet were still visible, curled and lifeless. I inquired about brown rice and was curtly told it was considered fodder for pigs. Again, we were grilled regarding our intentions and purpose, and our responses were just not striking the right chords. I was the one doing the responding, this was likely to have been the entire problem. A woman with the temerity to speak while the man who accompanied her sat silent was aberrant, and not to be trusted. I felt sorry for Bob, who only wanted to sit at the master's feet as a devotee.

There were flies in the curry and flies in the curd. Every meal consisted of fresh curd made from cow's milk, white bread, white rice, potato curry and occasional lentil dahl. The Indian food was tasty, and I so wanted less of the white stuff. At every meal, a beaming host unwrapped the loaves of white bread with great ceremony, and sought our enjoyment and appreciation, which was given unstintingly. New Yorkers have a culinary problem no matter where they travel. The great melting pot city has known wave after wave of immigration, authentic ethnic food made by authentic multinationals is available on every corner. I had been enjoying Indian food for years in New York and was anxious to experience the local cuisine. Instead, I smiled and sang the praises of white bread.

Clothing was the same. I wanted to learn to wrap the sari, to manage the undergarments and the blouse. What I really wanted was the jeweled hennaed feet and to waft sandalwood on the air as I walked by. My mother had raised me to believe that the ultimate signature of a woman was to be recognized by the perfumed scent that lingered after her. These women were queens, ranis of visual and olfactory delight. I wanted in.

Cultural differences again reigned. My sari lessons hit a stumbling block because I did not wear a bra. They had all been ceremonially burned to ashes in the late 1960s. Women had gathered on campus in enthusiastic groups, often led by our professors, to make their statement for gender equality. We tossed our bras into the fire, and cheered as the symbols of oppression ignited, one by one. In India, I was solemnly informed that I needed to go to town and purchase the boob holster. I refused, indignant, not about to don the yoke in a place where women were still treated as chattel.

The difficulties went on. The evening gatherings around Ram Chandra progressed, more English was spoken, and underlying attitudes began to emerge. That I traveled and shared a room with a man who was not my husband earned disapproval. That I spoke out and looked the men directly in the eye earned their uneasiness. The faux pas of foot reflexology, in the attempt to ease my ravaged digestion, led to pointed stares. I had not known that it was considered rude in Indian society to show one's feet. I tuned in to the conversation and listened as best I could, distracted by boredom and the vague hostilities. I often understood more than the men knew. Much can be gleaned by tonality, facial expression, and body language. As a child I had spent time with my grandfather in the deep South. After church, he would gather me up, buy me a huge candy bar, and "set" in a rocking chair on the porch of the general store in rural South Carolina. His buddy, Mr. Clinkscales, ran the establishment, a fascinating place full of candy bars and other wares displayed on wooden shelves. The rocking, smoking men spoke English, flavored with southern drawls which were nearly impenetrable to my northern ears. It was there that I learned to study expression, intonation, and body language for clues of meaning. Already a stranger in a strange land, I was no more than eight years old. I don't know why my grandfather picked this little girl to go visiting with him. He never spoke about it, but I like to think he recognized a kindred spirit. The son of two teachers, he had run away to sea as a youth, sailing the world on a merchant steamer. When he came back from

China, family legend says he returned with eyes that had "seen." When I finally got back home, my mother pronounced that I too had eyes that had "seen." I thank my grandfather, Robert Oscar Brantly, for the gifts of the wandering spirit which granted me destiny in the remote corners of the world.

It was a strange déjà vu to be sitting in the Indian evenings with these gentlemen who discoursed in Urdu. Monkeys appeared in the twilight, swinging across the courtyard, which I found enchanting. To the locals they were vermin, and they warned us to hide our jewelry. I admired the monkeys' abilities to swing with their fifth appendage, their tail. The windows of our room overlooked a tributary of the Ganges. Sometimes there were shepherds slowly driving flocks of water buffalo to the river, a timeless sight. Immersion in the Goddess River Ganga is thought to purify the soul and bring about the remission of all sins. To have one's ashes deposited in the Holy Ganges breaks the cycle of reincarnation and allows one direct connection with the Godhead. The sacred waters were a study of contrasts; the recipient of holy objects and veneration, where bumps below the surface emerged as crocodiles or unburned corpses. On weekends, we saw joyous wedding processions, loud brassy affairs with horns blowing and "captive" brides in red. Afternoons were for resting, full out horizontal, until the heat lifted enough to make movement bearable.

We meditated with Ram Chandra every morning, men on one side, women segregated on the other. Twenty or thirty people crowded into his small rooms. One morning I heard a flute outside his window by the river. It played on so sweetly and evocatively, it could have been the Lord Krishna himself. Session over, I headed to the window to look for the flautist. There was not a soul in sight, no human visible on the riverbanks for miles. It was inexplicable.

Physically feeling stronger, I decided to investigate the paper insert that was included with the bottle of reddish liquid I had been prescribed in Afghanistan. It was some sort of tonic to remediate my weakened state. To my vegetarian horror, my daily tonic contained the blood of Arabian horses! It always left my lips red, which may have been the artificial coloring, and the taste was sweet, but.... there I was, a drinker of animal blood, sitting at a Hindu holy man's feet!!

An Ayurvedic physician came to visit with his wife. He was tall and turbaned, with a flowing beard, dramatically handsome. She wore the Muslim dress of ankle-gathered pants under a long tunic. This man had none of the veiled contempt that the others had for us, and I found myself confiding about the stallion blood. He prescribed little lactose pills, which seemed rather insignificant, but would prove to be profound.

A journey into town was planned for a diversion and a chance to secure some cash. Long before ATMs, banking in a third world country was a complex process, rumored to be especially arduous in India. Horror stories described a four hour wait just do one transaction. We had to cash travelers' checks, nothing complicated. In India, armed guards stood sentry at the doorways of public places. This bank was no exception, with two men at attention, guarding the doorway with wicked eight-foot spears. Inside, we waited on endless lines for unavailable officials. When one finally arrived, he would sniff over our papers and send us to another unavailable official on another floor. The process repeated itself a dozen times until one man actually handwrote in our passports "Encash $50." Overall, our banking experience took more than five hours.

Wandering the colorful streets of Shahjahanpur later that day was a pleasure despite the heat. Posters from the Ramayana adorned the walls of the shopkeepers' stalls. The elephant god Ganesh and the monkey god Hanuman, representing incarnations of universal truths, were familiar as I meandered the marketplace, at ease and alone. Nikon in hand, I followed some goats ambling down a street near the market. The rains had come, there were large, deep puddles all around. I saw an oddity on the surface of the puddles, something I could not figure out. A dark spot resolved into two pieces of flesh, which became nostrils, as a giant hairy boar emerged from a puddle. It was the size of a German shepherd, with long hair and wicked tusks. It chased me a bit and then lost interest, going back to its waterhole to cool off. Local men paid no more attention than to turn their heads, busy as they were with loading cow chips onto the roofs of their dwellings. The dung, turned every few days, would dry in the brutal sun and soon be fuel for the household cook fires.

While I was framing up my photos, a crowd of young people had gathered around me. I paid them little heed, focused on the amusing antics of the photogenic goat. The first stone took me by surprise, a sharp stinging pain. Salvo after salvo was fired at me, hitting with increasing frequency. Tales of stonings in biblical times flashed into my head, and I began to panic, seeking a way out, finding none. The crowd had me surrounded. More stones struck, and harder. Suddenly an avenging angel appeared, Ram Chandra's grandson, yelling at the crowd, shaming them, dispersing them. He escorted me back to the compound, quietly angry and disdainful of this western woman whom circumstance had forced him to defend. I was bruised, shaken, but very much alive. No one at the compound so much as mentioned the incident. I had been warned not to venture into town without an escort. If I chose to risk my life, it was my own concern. It was clearly time to move on.

Kathmandu.... The Bob Seger lyrics [15] were rolling through my brain, I just wanted to be outta there, I couldn't get the words out of my head. At the evening soiree, the disapproval of my plans was immediate. I was so done with these fat and controlling men, their misunderstandings and criticisms. Later that night, I was invited to the room of the senior advisor's father to discuss the situation. I found it a bit odd, but hoped he was going to help me soothe roughened feathers. When I arrived, he began rambling about himself, his widower status, and his temptations. He said that the master knew about his weaknesses. Was he implying complicity? He actually inferred that there would be spiritual benefit for me to allow him to indulge himself. I was young enough to listen, but old enough to be sick at heart. He was trying very hard to be persuasive and I didn't have a good exit strategy. It was a stroke of good fortune when my friend Bob came inquiring after me, allowing for a quick departure.

The next morning, Ram Chandra, suddenly very fluent in English, told me of how some people came to his home and complained about him within his very walls. The words he used echoed my own. The man either had supernatural abilities or my confidences had been betrayed. When we sat down to meditate, I was hit by a burst of energy that knocked me out of my body. I could see myself sitting below, and light flickered all around me as I soared up and up, leaving my physical form and all abilities to record with my senses behind. I could say that I floated in endlessness, I could say that my consciousness merged with the universal mind, that I went to a place beyond space and time. There are no words for what happened. Much, much later, I became aware of the flickering light again, felt the sensation that I did not want to return, and then decelerated back into my body. When I could open my eyes, the master was standing right in front of me. He asked innocently "Was that better?" I had no speech to reply, no ability to form words or process language.

Cognition did not return for hours. I lay on my bed in the dormitory like a rag doll. That evening the master paid me special attention, talking about the mysteries of reincarnation, answering my questions, discoursing fondly about Gandhi. Ram Chandra (the name, literally, means "Servant of the Moon") said that Gandhi would reincarnate in London in his next life. He told a story of Gandhi being asked to arbitrate a Hindu/Muslim crisis in which a Hindu man came to visit him, full of contrition. The man had committed a violent act, dragging a Muslim who had threatened his family out of safety and killing him. At the time, the Hindu had felt justified, yet he came to Gandhi doubting and remorseful. The dead man had left behind a small son, the Hindu was childless. Gandhi charged the Hindu to raise the dead man's child with care and devotion "But, you must raise him as a Muslim."

Chapter

# 14

☷

# PALACE OF DREAMS

We took the night train back to Delhi, a real British leatherette sleeper car. I was resting comfortably when suddenly awakened by wrenching gut pain. The last of the Ayurvedic physician's little pills had run out. It was hard to believe that my recent well-being was due to the natural medicines, but apparently it was.

Our room, above a nightclub in Shahjahanabad, was a rat role in a residence hotel. It was still in Old Delhi, but a step up from our last place. There still was no toilet but a large chamber with a squatter was down the hall. Excrement covered the floor. To get across to the plumbing, one had to wade around ankle deep shit. My feet and pant legs had brown stains by the end of each day, requiring daily washing. The sun was strong and the heat so oven-like that cotton yoga pants dried in less than five minutes.

Rats climbed the tops of the walls, which did not meet the ceiling. They ran across the partitions, squealing, and occasionally scooted down a wall to bite one of the children. A ceiling fan hung suspended by just one wire, spinning. Horizontal from the intense press of the heat, I would watch the fan idly while trying to nap, wondering if this was the moment that the wire would snap and hurl the rotating blades into my abdomen. Why did I tolerate such conditions? Because I was determined not to be a tourist, because I was here to experience the culture and conditions as they were presented to me. There was pride and community in being an overlander, part of the "sandals on the ground" backpacking set who did not want to buy their way into an artificial experience. We wanted to meet the conditions as they were, hopefully without too many judgments. That was the hard part, not the trying physical conditions. It was easy to be judgmental, as a westerner from far easier physical circumstances. It was common to be judged, as a foreigner who might look outlandish or behave unacceptably. None of it was admirable.

So I lay on the bed in a downtrodden part of a steaming Indian city, writing poetry and prose to a lost love, contemplating my next moves. I was feeling unwell, and Pennsylvania Bob, my traveling companion for the last many leagues, was bailing out. Steve the Brit had reappeared, last seen on the trail in Herat. He was noticeably thinner and making haste back to London. He told of a stay in a local hospital, where the food and linens had to be supplied by family. Having no family closer than Devonshire, Steve lay in the soiled sheets of the last man in that bed and went hungry while his mysterious eye condition was being investigated. Once released, he was wasting no time in making his escape. Kathmandu beckoned to me, just up the road, but a sense of foreboding created a cloud of uncertainty. I pointed my face to the sun, hoping the darkness would fall behind.

Outside, the magic of timeless India was delicate, ethereal. Rajasthan, lavish in architecture and artistic history, was long ruled by warrior kings who esteemed the arts as much as they did battle. Medieval Agra called, the Taj Mahal glowing in perfect alabaster symmetry against a white-hot Indian sky. Its lines, all curving turrets and towering minarets, transported one to a less corporeal age and time. The massive monument to love built by Shah Jahan for his beloved Mumtaz was cool marble vista upon cool marble vista. Footwear forbidden, I marveled at the delicious feel of the rock under my feet in the oppressive heat. Thousands of pairs of sandals waited outside to be reclaimed in an orderly fashion. The pervasive tranquility permeating the Taj soothed and polished the rough edges of humanity with calm.

We journeyed. Fatepuhr Sikri, the haunted city, loomed above me like a hungry incubus sucking for sustenance. Built by the Mughal emperor Akbar to honor the Sufi mystic Salim Chishti, Akbar had the massive gates and sprawling red sandstone palaces built after the sheik's fertility invocation yielded three sons for the royal line. In the general fervor to honor the saint for the blessing of sons, his advisors failed to notice that the desert plain upon which they sited the city was waterless. They created an architectural masterpiece, which thirst forced them to abandon short decades later. Outside the seat of the court astrologer, the faithful offered prayers at the Mazar of Sheik Salim, threads tied at the marble windows floating translucent on the scalding breeze.

I was at home in Akbar's personal palace and climbed on his great sandstone bed. The tales were of royal passions, murders, vengeance, and fratricide. The palace offered sweeping vistas, fountains and pools, flowing water streaming by in cooling currents. Alabaster pillars, carved and painted exquisitely with birds and flowers, still looked enchanting despite the theft of their precious jewels. As I wandered through the open-air residence, a caressing wind sprang up. I meandered through the rooms in solitude, certain of their layout, knowing what was coming next before it appeared. The fountains sang for me, sweet birdsong a melody as I floated on gossamer gusts. Endorphins flooded through me, wave after wave of biochemical bliss. I knew the views, the varied vistas, the sounds of slippered feet as the eunuchs stole down the hallways bent on their mysterious errands. Below, the gazing pool and its four bridges tickled the familiar like ghosts of my grandparents' summer home, on faraway Paumanok Island, on the other side of the world. Reclining under the open sky, I gave myself over to the sensations playing me like the strings of a harp. Only much later was I reclaimed by the twentieth century. Fatepuhr Sikri, now a UNESCO World Heritage site, was designed after the Masjid-Al –Haram in Al Makkah. My journey to Mecca was two years in the future; at that time, I could only think of Sir Richard Burton's. The 19th century linguist, proto anthropologist and explorer had penetrated the inner sanctum of Mecca in disguise, for the penalty for an infidel found near the Ka'aba was death. Hâjî Abdû El-Yezidî, the Sufi identity that he assumed, lived to describe the holiest sanctum of Islam. Was it just recollections of his traveler's tales that stirred the serpent to rise up my spine? Was it so much more?

Back in the city, caste was readily apparent in the stream of humanity on the streets. It wasn't just that the poor were barefoot or skinny or maimed. They were emaciated small-boned women and men, very dark-skinned, with shiny jet-black hair and Caucasian features. The privileged continued to parade their wealth as body fat. Only a person with an abundance of food to eat could possibly have enough excess calories to store. Zaftig upper caste women walked the bazaars, rolls of belly fat hanging proudly from beneath their midriff tops. The longing and envy were tangible as the poor cut their covetous eyes to the proud and pendulous flesh.

Lovely Lakshmi of the Lotus drifted down the staircase bedecked in a gilded red sari and hip length hair. I thought I had never seen such beautiful women as lived in our hotel. It was a residence for nightclub entertainers, females of arresting beauty and sensuality, hennaed and painted and bejeweled. One evil evening, after darkness had stolen down, the acid voice of an American man rent the air, assaulting a woman and her small child. In a southern accent, raging drunk, he launched a stream of venom, denouncing the boy as a monkey for his Indian looks and dark skin. The racist invective tore at the screaming child, as the beast rained blows on mother and son. What to do, what to do? There were no authorities to call in this teeming third world city. Resolving to help, I walked into the hallway. The man's maddened ranting filled the night. I saw other women standing silently in the shadows, listening, all of us paralyzed by the force of the hatred, the bitter blows, the terrified screams of the child. We stood under the moon, a sisterhood of sorrow; helpless, tears streaming down faces. In the morning, the mother brought out the boy, he of the huge staring eyes, unresponsive to tenderness or sweet speech. We women gathered, cooing, stroking and soothing in one soprano voice in the hopes that our song could heal.

I didn't feel well enough to continue onward in Asia. I needed medical treatment in a familiar western setting. Syrian Arab Airlines was the ticket out. The hostile man I sat next to, attired in turban and traditional garb, dug into the meal served between Delhi and Teheran with gusto. I couldn't stomach the food, bent double as I was in a wrenching agony of gut pain and weakness. Flying west reversed the 1,600-mile overland trek through the burning deserts in an astonishingly short time frame. Landing in Teheran, I sat aboard the plane and prayed for the strength to make it back to the world I knew. If I had to be carried off here, I was still in the midst of the deserts, and although the medical care in Teheran might be adequate with the Shah's westernization, I craved the security of a familiar world. The next leg took us to Damascus and the meal was the first recognizable food I had seen in months. Mustering the strength to swallow a few bites, I watched the man next to me. Mystified by cherry tomatoes, he chased them around his plate in unsuccessful attempts to spear the unfamiliar. An eight-hour layover became twelve, and then sixteen. I could barely lift my head out of my lap by then and was in abject terror of not making it out of Syria. The Damascus airport was just Quonset huts, a quasi-military spartan outpost in the desert. A military commander roared up in a jeep with a large gun mounted on its hood. He stood, imperiously commanding the scene, arrogant lines of cruelty etched into his face. Inside, he cast his intimidating gaze upon each passenger, demanding documents. As his attentions made their way closer towards me, I caved. My head was buried in my lap, praying that the antagonistic commandant would pass me by. Something heard. He did.

I watched a wall clock tick away the hours, imploring the heavens for safety. When our Zurich-bound DC-7 became airborne, my genes began encoding hope. In a few short hours, I could be in Europe. Safe. Assured of survival. I agonized the air miles, checking land masses out of the window, willing the barren desert to transform into green. With no guarantee of where I was, I made myself rehearse a mental scenario of being hospitalized in Iran or Turkey, and the thoughts of the conditions in Kurdistan or Iraq below tortured me. We got socked in by cloud cover, nothing more could be seen. Again and again, anticipating futility, I laboriously raised my head to gaze out the window.

One magic moment, there stood the Alps, gray granite peaks piercing the clouds in majesty, announcing the security of the western world was mine. Was it Mont Blanc or the Matterhorn that hove its head that day to announce that I had attained the Holy Grail? No matter, they are both revered in memory now. Forevermore, the Alps are my sanctuary, a cherished safe haven of home.

Chapter

# 15

☰

# LONDON AND COPPETT'S WOOD

L ondon in August: no room at the inn. There wasn't a hotel vacancy in the entire city. After hours of fruitless search, we finally found a small rooming house an hour away in the suburbs. The journey to it required three trains; my new-found energy, the product of my elation, waned. When Bob and I arrived, landlady took one look at me and suddenly nothing was available. Utterly dejected, I sat on the stairs, unable to stand. I couldn't carry my backpack; my legs had turned to water again. Perhaps the Indian sandals and ankle bracelets were too much for her. My feet weren't hennaed, they were just stained from months of trudging the trail in sandals. I hadn't even noticed in India, where the heat had necessitated four showers a day. I told my friend that I couldn't do it, couldn't go any farther, and could not get back on the train. My despair must have softened the eavesdropping innkeeper, for she allowed us a room in her airless attic for forty-five dollars. I crawled up the stairs on my hands and knees and did not leave the bed for thirty-six hours.

Feeling considerably better, my next and nearly last adventure had me out and about in London. The optimistic plan was to recover for a few days and then head up to Scotland. My maternal grandmother was a MacDougall, with Menzies and Fraser blood. The MacDubhgalls had once been puppet kings of the northern isles under the Norse. Perhaps after the Scottish Highlands, I would visit the Orkney homelands. I just had to get Asia out of my guts.

After my long rest, I left the rooming house to meet up with an American acquaintance who was house-sitting an artists' flat in Kent. The flat's owners, sculptors both, were on holiday in Greece. The rooms were full of life-sized figures with purple hair and grotesque green faces. The bedroom, however, was regal, with a black and gold platform bed displayed in a grand style. Following dinner with new friends and a few drinks, I returned late to the flat. It was to be my last coherent act for some days. The alcohol had done its work, I was physically destroyed. Raising my head off the pillow caused waves of dizziness and nausea. I lay fevered in sweat-soaked sheets, unconscious much of the time. When I did rouse, it took all of my effort to roll onto a dry spot in the bed. Uncharacteristically, I did not speculate what was going to happen to me, I had no mental energy at all.

Sometimes I woke to pitch blackness, other times, to bright sun. In the darkness I fancied that I heard those leering statues with the terrible faces coming toward the bedroom. Sometimes I awoke to the horrible Hannibal-type creatures gathered about the bed, murmuring and watching. Was it just the delirium? When my friend returned after a few days, I do remember being disappointed that she was departing immediately. I had had nothing to eat or drink for days, she fixed me something and bolted in mortal fear of contagion. I heard a promise to call a doctor as the door slammed.

I lay on the floor of the living room, waiting for the telephone to ring, and passed out from the effort of getting there. My head had to stay on the floor, or else my senses would scramble to the point where I couldn't sort anything and I would shut down. The doctor who called heard my incoherence paired with the word "India" and said that an ambulance would be coming straightaway. Now my task was to not be unconscious when it arrived. I went in and out of awareness, sometimes a person lying on a floor of a surreal flat in England, sometimes nowhere at all. I wondered if that was what death was.

Noise at the door. I heaved myself along the floor on hands and knees. Got the door open just in time to see the ambulance men climbing back into their vehicle. They brought a stretcher when they saw me, but oddly, refused to help me climb on to it. They weren't too happy about handling my backpack, either. Neighbors began to appear to see the spectacle, silent watchers, I was used to that. One foot and one hand a time, falling over to the ground a lot, I willed myself to crawl onto that stretcher. The men lifted it in and shut the doors. I was under way to help.

They whispered "India" and I heard "It's cholera, man, it's cholera." I lay on the gurney and watched the chimney pots of London go by, all double chimneys. Looking around, I realized that everything had gone double now, my eyes could no longer hold a focus. I lay on the gurney and watched the chimney pots of London go by, all double chimneys......

When we got to Coppetts Wood hospital, I was expected to walk down a corridor to a room. I tried hard, observed by a crew of hospital personnel who had come out to attend the arrival of a foreigner newly out of Asia with some abominable tropical disease. I bounced off the walls, unable to maintain linear forward motion. Then came bed, and total collapse. There was no intake, no paperwork, no ER, just a glass-walled cubicle with a window and a lidded bedpan under a chair. This was an English national health service infectious disease and isolation hospital. I was so happy to be there. I placed my survival in the hands of the doctors and nurses. Later, the bedpan told the story. Snow-white stool, shiny like plastic, with urine the color of blood. Hepatitis.

In the morning, a male nurse arrived with what appeared to be a small rocket under his arm. He threaded a needle into it and proceeded to draw off most of my blood volume! Then I was wheeled outside, head bobbing weakly, for a chest x-ray on a glorious English summer afternoon. I quietly vomited into one of those kidney-shaped plastic hospital dishes. Hospital food in England was just as unappetizing as at home, but somehow I was hungry. I looked at the boiled mystery meat and cold potatoes. A vegetarian for four years, I wondered what that meant now, after my grand trip to India. I closed my eyes and took a bite. Instantaneously, my gorge rose in my throat and the taste of pork overwhelmed me. The vomit sprayed across the whole bed, over and over and over, but the taste never went away. Vomiting became a way of life. I probably only brought up substance twenty-five times a day, but I was in a state of permanent retch. I tasted pork for ten days.

I cried between episodes, but crying took energy, and there was precious little of that. The room spun constantly, just lifting my head could incite another round of gut-wrenching gagging. My back began to ache, endlessly. I found a football-sized concavity in the mattress and asked for another. Instead, I was offered muscle relaxants. I was angry. My impaired liver hardly needed to be called upon to process a drug! Functional medicine associates overworked liver function with anger, and I was one wrathful hospital detainee. I held my ground: no drugs, new mattress. The situation necessitated a visit from "Sister," the head nurse, who denounced my unreasonable demand in no uncertain terms. I was unmovable. The next day, I had another mattress.

Each morning, the staff would wash my body with hot water. My liver, normally housed under the right ribs, had swelled left across my midsection and was heading south towards my right ovary. It made strange gurgling sounds. An iridescent orange color, spilling bile pigments, spread across my abdomen in a growing stain. A full third of my body was neon orange. At five feet seven- and three-quarter inches, I would leave the hospital weighing ninety-eight pounds. I listened to the staff talking as they hand-washed bedpans in the sluice just down the hall from my room. It was the hottest English summer in eighteen years, about eighty-five degrees, and the kind nurse who tended me suffered in the heat, her English Rose cheeks in high bloom. The aides who washed me gawked at my orangeness and my bony emaciation. My hips stuck out like the scapulae of starving cows on the streets of Delhi. I was a rare enough creature that a parade passersby looked in my window constantly. I pulled down the window shade, they pulled it up again, complaining and scolding.

The doctor told me that I had a particularly bad kind of hepatitis, salmonella typhi, and amoebic dysentery. He wanted to know why everyone coming off the overland trail to India was sick. How could I begin to explain to this proper English gentleman about wading through piles of shit every day? About reaching for the pitcher to pour with your right, wipe with your left, and finding that your hand was brown? What about the typhoid vats in Afghanistan, where great cauldrons of sheep's milk were slow heated over a fire for hours, the perfect growth medium for killer tubercles? For tea there was water from the drainage ditches, which men crouched over each morning to deposit their bowel movements. Should I tell him of the tea sellers who rushed to those same ditches to fill their kettles? How about the black flies zooming off the dung heaps directly into your mouth? It was the frontier, but instead of the arid west, it was the steaming tropics. Still, in a world without the concepts of germs and contagion, did germs and contagion really exist? Were their intrinsic properties altered by their lack of recognition resonance in the environment? Quantum physics says that we alter the nature of reality just by perceiving it, or not. I wanted to explore these points with the Anglican minister who made a courtesy call at my cubicle. I wanted to discuss the ideas of Hinduism and Christianity and Islam and Judaism. He said a polite "Good morning" and bailed. I heard him heartily discussing soccer scores next door. Profound discussion was clearly not his forte.

My friend Bob came to visit. He was shocked by my appearance, regretful, avid for his next day departure back to the USA. He promised to call my parents, we said we would keep in touch, and then he, too, was history.

The vertigo was what made it all unbearable. The slightest movement of my head would set it off. Dizzy and disoriented, waves of vomiting would carry me away. My secret solution was Dramamine. Motion sickness had haunted me as a child, this was eerily similar. I chewed a quarter of a pill from my backpack. It worked! I could not tell the staff, after all my outraged noise about their muscle relaxants. The ocean of heaving waves that had buffeted me for weeks began to calm. At night I heard a comforting humming around me. It lulled me to sleep like a mother's song. In reality, my mother had called together a healing circle for me, they had gathered in my name and were sending me energy. The first night that I heard the sounds turned out to be the first night that they had gathered together! In the words of William James, "Never close your accounts with reality." (16)

It was three more weeks before I got out of the hospital. I left without permission. Even with my English Rose sneaking me chocolate bars, I could not handle another day of that place. My urine came back triple negative, indicating that I was no longer contagious, and the next day I was outta there.

Onward to Devonshire, to my friend Stephen, whose mother thought I had come to marry him. Once she got over that notion, we got on quite well. I rested there for a few weeks, and then steamed up the Elbe back to Hamburg and the one I had left behind. Christian took me to a farm in Schleswig-Holstein, near Denmark. I convalesced, lying in a cow pasture watching NATO jet maneuvers in the blue sky, eating fresh antimicrobial garlic and homemade cheese. On to the city of Hamburg itself, bunking with literary types in a fourth-floor walkup whose stairs kept me inside reading their collection of great American writers, Baldwin and Hemingway, Chandler and Hammett.

After a month in Germany, I moved on to Denmark's copper clad capital of Kobenhavn. It was a magical place, where descendants of Vikings with blonde braids as thick as my wrist were clad in velvets, drinking beer. I walked the winter twilight streets of Copenhagen to build my strength. The stone-cold city of the north held a certain fascination. Wooden shop signs creaked in the chill wind. Every day at four PM, the bakeries brought out steaming butter-rich pastries for the crowds who lined up at their doors. The season changed, and daylight was a feeble thing, lasting no more than three hours. Streets were lit up twenty-four/seven, homes were too. The Danes counterpunched the tide of rising darkness with color. It seemed every woman was a fine knitter. When the cold came on with the darkness, every person on the walking streets sported brightly colored knitted caps and mittens. The faces were mesmerizing, high Asiatic cheekbones below eyes of startling blue, skin like new milk, and eight shades of blonde hair. Living in Jutland on the west coast, I one day discovered a hole in my boots. Had I been walking the Norse lands for too long? It was

December, I had been gone almost a year. Time to dash away home to New York.

Chapter

# 16

≣

# FLIGHT SCHOOL-
# JOHN F. KENNEDY
# INTERNATIONAL AIRPORT 1977

The sky was calling. When the big envelope came from the international airline, I knew I was in. It had been a roller coaster; the previous week, getting the "we regret we are no longer hiring" letter after two excellent interviews. Now this. I could feel a huge shift coming in my life. I was moving onward, to international flight attendant school at JFK.

Friends were very enthused. They had seen me stagger shell-shocked back from Middle East and struggle to regain my bearings. Then the dark wings of fate had descended, my mother dying in my arms, breaking my heart and crushing my spirit. Can any experience be more devastating than the loss of one's mother, the source of life itself? The loss of a child can be, miscarriage, the neonatal ICU, but those threats were in a then-unknown future.

I had returned in time to nurse my mother through her unsuccessful battle with one of the deadliest cancers. I had given her great hope simply because I could not fathom that she could really die. Die she did, while I held her, brokenly asking us (her husband, sister, and daughter) to let her go. "Someone is holding me here," she whispered, "You must let me go…. I have to go……. release me." A Christian, she drew herself up into the cross, and murmured, "I freely release myself and let me go to my highest good." Her last words were "He's here," meaning Christ… and then she was gone. Her eyes held a vision of something incomprehensible and vast. I stared into her open eyes, trying to decipher where she was, wanting her to see me still, but I was impotent in the face of the Great Mystery, and my mother's eyes would never look into mine again. I mourned, for the ending of her life and that relationship in which I was loved in a foundational, and unconditional fashion. There were rivers of tears. Then came the big envelope. It had hope, glamour, adventure, and a quality of fantasy. I was reinventing my life. People stood when I walked into the room.

It was Hendrix who said "'Scuse me- while I kiss the sky."[17] Before any strikes on the stratosphere could occur, rigorous military-style training in emergency procedures had to be endured; first aid, evacuations, hijackings, water landings, and more. Concurrently, memorization of insane lists of equipment and airport codes was required, a score of less than 75 on any test meant you were going home. The first weeks saw a rash of sorrowing young adults, including my roommate, shamefacedly packing their bags. Most of my classmates were in their early twenties, fresh out of college, untried. The pressure was grueling, the instructors hard, uncompromising women; they demanded obedience, strict punctuality, and mastery of detail. Saluting and clicking one's heels were a plus. The grooming instructor, who had police powers, rated our outfits daily for fashion impact, the scale her constant threat.

Fortunately, a friend whose mother owned a modeling agency had taken me under her stylish wing. She loaned me outfits, took me shopping and generally spiffed up the Birkenstock babe. The attrition rate was remarkably high as survivors of the program struggled to keep up with its rigors and regrouped after unexpected departures. We wanted to succeed very badly; the lure of the lifestyle was intoxicating. We learned aircraft designs, and how to operate oxygen systems, vital in case of emergency. Evacuation procedures required extensive drilling, with just 2.5 minutes to get 252 passengers and ten crew out of the aircraft and far away. Jumping onto the safety chutes brought inevitable injuries as speed was all. We role-played panicked passengers, drunks, medical emergencies, and hijackings.

Ditchings and hijackings were perhaps the most threatening situations that a flight attendant could face then, other than the very rare and inevitably fatal mid-air collisions. Accidents on the ground were often survivable, we were so well drilled that responding became rote. Few survived a water landing; the life raft scenario, with its flares and desalinization kits, was intimidating. We watched films simulating an infamous ditching in the Caribbean, where two out of three survivors were picked off by sharks. There followed a serious discussion of shark psychology.

Hijackings were a significant and frequent threat. This was the heyday of Cuban cowboys co-opting aircraft for their political agendas. A spunky little stew with jujitsu training showed up to demonstrate holds and hand-to-hand evasive maneuvers, as if we would learn them in one session. We were taught to rely on the cockpit for aid. The almighty captain would burst through the door, sword in hand, and overpower the terrorists with his august presence. Or maybe he would descend through the clouds immediately for the authorities to save us from our peril.

Perhaps because I was a few years older, or perhaps for other reasons, I was picked to handle the worst crisis situations in the role-plays. Unbeknownst to the instructors, I had been a crisis intervention counselor, having worked in a community "hotline" facility for suicide and drug abuse. My years of traipsing the barrios and the bowels of Manhattan in search of parents who had abandoned their kids to foster care also stood me in good stead. I had a tendency for careful observation in new situations. I couldn't be provoked to lose it in crisis, and I scored perfectly on the medical certification tests, a harbinger of things to come. What no one knew was that I had a real fear of deep water, and we were about to be forced to ditch in the deep.

Our next challenge was to be taken out into the Atlantic for water landing simulations. Rough water, open seas, bobbling life rafts, controlled panic. Frankly, I was terrrrified. It wasn't doable. I called my father, preparing him for my exit. Many others made anxious calls home. My friend Walt, ever confident, blew off the drama, telling me to just hold my nose and jump in.

The word came down that we would have our trial in an Olympic-sized swimming pool which would be churned up to simulate rough water. The first concern of almost everyone was how they would be rated in a bathing suit! The competition was not among us as much as between us and the training personnel, who threw people out of the program seemingly on a whim. What about a little jiggle on the thighs? Blemishes or big butts? Everyone had their particular insecurities, we sat around discussing the horrifying possibilities. I for one knew I could not go through with a simulation out in the ocean; at least this next step was in the realm of possibility. I would endure these bathing suit trials for another chance to get my wings. I was standing in the saddle; the brass ring was nearly within reach.

The first tests were easy, treading water, swimming set distances. Then we were loaded onto life rafts and told to prepare to be thrown over the side in a backwards roll, upside down, head over heels. There were multiple rafts, trainers with stop watches blowing whistles, splashing water, screams and tears. One had a fixed number of seconds to make it to the surface and swim to the side of the pool. Mess it up, and you were out on your wet and sorry ass. I witnessed the sobbing hysteria of those who failed to make it, amidst the whistles and pandemonium.

I clung to the back of the life raft, watching others go overboard. Soon it would be my turn, I felt paralyzed with fear. There were two men throwing people to their doom. I chose Michel, a soft-spoken black man who had always seemed kind. Getting into the preparation stance, felt him reach for me, and utterly froze. I just could not do it, knew I would go down in a panic, choking on water and never making it up on time. "I can't!" I yelled, and he nodded, allowing me to back off and collect myself. The other man loomed, with a fixed focus, I blocked him out. There was only me, Michel, and the water. If I wanted this, and I surely knew I did, I had to become airborne and crash land in the water upside down. Michel kept tossing bodies, looked over at me, and I gave him the sign. We were in this together. I held my nose and closed my eyes as I flew over backwards, hit the water and in an instant was kicking it for the edge of the pool. I barely raised an eyebrow from the instructors. I was in.

Leaving the pool with my friend Rosary, who had the best legs in the class, we drew stares and I concentrated on making my trembling rubber limbs propel forward motion. That night brought a champagne celebration up on the roof, toasts to our upcoming adventures and liberation, and the cementing of a life-long friendship. Rosary was a Jersey girl, who loved the Shore and Bruce Springsteen. Her Dad had been in the construction business, I thought perhaps making concrete boots. She had lost her father to an early heart attack, our shared grief for our lost favorite parent was the first bond between us. In class, she stood up for the introductions in a seersucker suit with a red scarf tied around her neck and said something saucy. I sought her out immediately, sensing a kindred spirit. We became confidantes, sidekicks, and road-buddies.

The airport hotel was multistoried with a flat roof. Situated within the JFK airport complex, it lay on a final approach pattern which was in frequent use. The couples who had hooked up in class discovered that the roof was a great spot for nocturnal activities. We all had roommates, so privacy was hard to come by. The best thing about rooftop rendezvous was viewing the underbellies of the jets. The big birds soared only a few hundred feet above, gear down, flaps set, screaming in for a landing only moments away. It was a huge adrenalin rush, a sexual enhancement, and it was almost our time to hit the sky. We drank more Dom Perignon to the promise.

The next phase of the program was cake; galley duty, meal service, management of the liquor cart, how to cope with turbulence, the duties of each flight attendant position on the aircraft, and that oxymoron, "cockpit etiquette." Our confidence growing, so too was the inevitable experimentation of young women and men about to leap out of a pressure cooker and into the fast lane. Parties and juicy times abounded, it was sex and drugs and rock n' roll, although I passed on the ménage a trois. The excitement level was through the roof and the heady sense of imminent breakthrough of the boundaries of our lives was intoxicating.

I was living in an old Gold Coast mansion on the north shore of Long Island, less than an hour from JFK. We had fourteen acres, a private beach on the waterfront, and a host of avant garde artistes to fill the eight bedrooms. We also had some of the best parties in known history. It was there that I brought my flight attendant pals on the weekends, and among them was Walt. Walt was a golden gregarious guy with enough wattage to melt icebergs. He was smooth but he was also sincere, and always on the pulse of what was happening. It was Walt who spotted the romantic potential of the roof, and Walt who smoothed our way by soothing the ruffled feathers of the alpha females who decided our fate. His easy slide and glide manner and his propensity for good times was impressive. Walt's main squeeze, Sheri, was a cute little brunette from the Midwest whose giant breasts incited fantasy. On her maiden flight, her first captain had her perched on his lap. Things like that really did happen, and more than occasionally. The hottest captains would prove to be former Vietnam fighter pilots, politically conservative but physically appealing in their uniforms and wings. A hot captain was the epitome of cool. Most were married, but many were available, married or not.

I was late getting back to JFK for our observation flight. When I got to the hotel, Walt was pacing. "International traveler! Shows up with five minutes to spare!" he barked. Then we all flew off to London, working part of the way, whereupon I learned to pop champagne at 35,000 feet without causing a decompression and how to pour coffee during turbulence with no first-degree burns. I tried on a British accent and fooled the passengers for the whole trip home. My friends at the Mansion listened to our trans-Atlantic conversation about "hopping the pond" with openmouthed awe. A legend grew.

It was on my observation flight that I had my first heart-stopping glimpse of a captain named John, who stopped me in my tracks. I was sitting alone at breakfast when suddenly I saw him in silhouette. He stood in uniform in the rose garden of the Gatwick Hilton, smoking a cigarette with an easy grace. The sunlight illuminated the four bars which sat proudly on each of his shoulders. I knew with an utter certainty that we would meet again. And the following spring, in a charming old Paris hotel, we did.

Graduation day dawned. Our oppressors were suddenly our best friends, we had proved ourselves and made the grade. "Glamorous Gloria" emceed the ceremonies, gushing about the adventurous lives that awaited us now that we had earned the right to be free of gravity. Her dramatic finish was "And now---I give you--THE WORLD!" and she pinned each of us with a set of silver wings. I must admit, the wings felt literal. I was still in my twenties, had been *there and back again*, and had no responsibilities other than my own growth and happiness. I had read Castaneda and believed that we all create our own realities. Who knew what was out there? I pondered free will, recalling Psychology 101 debates about heredity vs. environment. In my early college days, I had been a champion of free will and nurture vs. nature. But I had been to India. The men who swung their legless bodies after me down the streets, the beggared and deformed multitudes, the white-eyed ones, staring blind and sightless, were living examples of karma. I considered myself so fortunate to be where I was, not to mention where I was going. Onward. I threw us a big graduation party at the Mansion, where we awaited our first assignment.

A crowd camped out at my house in anticipation of those phone calls from crew scheduling. Few had local accommodations yet, and we were facing "A" day, and the stress of a possible one-hour notice for showtime at the airport. "B" day gave us twelve hours, and "C" day, 24. The phone rang, Sheri was off to Ireland and her rendezvous with the captain who had her warm his lap. Walt got a trip to Switzerland; Rosary got the nod for Paris. The call that came for me told that I would work a trip to Rome, "float" for two days, awaiting another crew at the hotel, and then return out of Athens.

"Float" in Rome? I was ready, baby. I grabbed my wings and my wheels.

# Global

Chapter

# 17

☲

# THE HAJJ: GONE IN GHANA

he Hajj. The dream assignment, a month based in Africa, flying the Muslim faithful to their pilgrimage in Mecca. I bid the Hajj with little hope of getting the line, I was simply too junior to hold a bid that was so highly desired. One either loved the Hajj, the month-long assignment based in Africa flying to Jeddah airport, or one hated it. Those adventurous souls seeking the exotic and possessed of enough seniority were awarded the bid every year. Universally, a first-year person was discouraged from even trying for it. I took a chance. When the bid lines, the monthly trip schedules awarded by seniority, were posted, I saw regretfully that I wasn't even close.

I took off for Rome, where I had a five-day trip. We often took charters into Ciampino airport. The first time landing there, I exited the aircraft and was met by the sight of the Seven Hills of Rome. I sat on the portable stairs after the passengers had deplaned, basking in the warm golden light and taking in the terracotta tones of the hills. The earth, rust and sienna, radiated a richness, the purple shadows deep in the torpor of the late afternoon. I was transfixed. The limo took us along the Via Appia and with a jolt, I realized I was riding the ancient Appian Way of the Romans! We passed fields of amber crops, golden grains, grapevines, every tiled terracotta roof baking in the sun. The hotel even had a view of Il Coloseo. The Coliseum was smaller than I expected but richly vibrating with ancient echoes. I went there every time I went to Rome, sitting along in the stone seats, imagining the spectacles and the roar of the crowd. I went to Italy as frequently as I could, often to the lake district of the north, sometimes to Roma or Sicilia or Venezia. It fed my soul.

I returned home to a telegram from the chief flight attendant, congratulating me on being awarded the Hajj. The "dark continent" awaited me after all! I had seventeen days to pull it together. Through a fortuitous combination of flight attendants with the flu and others disenchanted by the particular bases chosen that year, my bid was taken. I went out to purchase a recording device that worked on foreign electrical current. The hip and handsome store clerk asked assumingly if I were going to Europe. "No, Africa," I said, and all conversation stopped. I noted the power of the word.

Immunizations were necessary, yellow fever and malaria and other dangers lurked. Guidelines were provided on how to dress and behave in the lands of Islam, frankly discouraging the wearing of revealing clothing or the demonstration of affection in public. No midriff tops, no shorts or bare legs, no behaving like an Ugly American. Photos of strangers were also prohibited, we were going to a land where there were animist beliefs about having one's soul stolen by an image, and violent incidents were not unknown. A telephoto lens was a must.

Three crews of thirteen flew off to Africa together, with an entire aircraft to spread ourselves into, no passengers on board. It was to be a seventeen-hour journey. The first few hours were spent in a limo from New York to Philadelphia. Then came a flight to the Azores, in the middle of the Atlantic, well west of Spain. They are the tiny tops of a mighty underwater mountain chain, miniscule volcanic tips peeping above the crashing ocean deeps. Our last leg took us from the Azores to Accra in Ghana, on a four-hour flight path over the Sahara.

The view was outstanding. There were no clouds, no water vapor, nothing to obstruct the sight of the rolling sand dunes 28,000 feet below. Possessed of eagle eyes, and better than 20/10 vision, with study I was able to spot caravans moving across the desert. I could just make out the camels as they dotted their way across the vast white shifting abyss. With relentless observation, I was actually able to spot the bending of the camels' knees. Their oasis destinations were diminutive dots of darkness in the burning glare. Viewed from that vantage, the Sahara is an ocean, you know, an ocean of blinding light. Giant wind-blown waves of sand drift in currents across the shifting face of eternity. After hours of persistent gazing, at an air speed of more than six hundred miles per hour, it seemed to me that the Sahara went on without end. It was a whole universe unto itself, remote and unknowable. How could that white sand world feel to someone moving through its relentless heat and glare on camel back, with animal stench in their nostrils and their body's life moisture parching out into the howling winds? Eternity was too small a concept.

Landing in Ghana's capitol Accra, we were met by the blackest people I had ever seen. All American blacks were café-au-lait in comparison. It made sense, given the burning intensity of the sun's rays here. Genes for light skin coloring were not acquired until Homo sapiens mated with Neanderthals after migration out of Africa. These sub-Saharan Africans would have been disadvantaged by those genes. The men, who were aircraft cleaners, stood on the tarmac in their white uniforms, an arresting sight. We must have looked exotic to them too, we all stood around gaping at each other open-mouthed until the senior stewardess took charge. She divided up the booty, distributing leftover alcohol, sodas and food from the trip. This occurred at the end of every terminal flight, spoils chosen by seniority. The cleaners got included in the process this time, after the crew. It brought offers to exchange currency at black market rates. The local currency, the cedi, was offered at a rate four times better than the official exchange. Many hesitated, milling about, unfamiliar with how it was done. No one but a neophyte would exchange their dollars at the officially published rate anywhere outside of Europe. I changed some money, and as I suspected, even better rates were available once we found our way around. The cleaners weren't dumb, they had gotten six packs of soda, not Scotch.

The route to the hotel took us along the crashing Atlantic by twilight; turquoise breakers and beached fishing boats dotted the deserted shore. Tall coconut palms swayed in the wind, laden with fruits that fell onto the sands. Quickly, it grew dark. The bus windows were open wide as we raced along the newly built coastal highway, the moon rising, our hair whipping in our eyes, shouting in excitement to our seatmates. The very air steamed with the rich ripeness of the continent. Forever I will know the smells of equatorial Africa borne on a warm wind. Imagine a land that never gets cold. The soil's flora and fauna were always ripe, pungent, never dormant as in lands that freeze down for long months at a time. Avocado and papaya and sweet mango fell from the trees to lie in fermenting heaps on the ground. The mighty three-headed Volta raced to the Bay of Guinea along banks of heated sandstone. Much of the coast lay below sea level, thickly forested with palms. The shoreline was pristine, undeveloped, access to the interior only by river boat or small aircraft. There was just the one coastal highway to Togo in the east. The winds blew from the south in the equatorial "winter," from the ocean deeps across the savannah. In summer, winds blew down from the Sahara, dry and laden with thick red dust.

Fishing was the major livelihood. The men put out to sea at night in their hand painted wooden pirogues, their women often met them in the water when the sun rose to bring in the catch. The seafarers spread their nets to dry in the hot sun before going home to sleep. The boats lay quiet in the heat of the day, the beaches deserted. The sea was a rare turquoise, all the more striking by contrast with the rich green vegetation which grew to the water's edge. A fierce and constant undertow besieged the shoreline, eating away at the soft rock and devouring sandy banks.

In the heart of the city, bare-breasted women bore goods on their heads, sometimes piled more than three feet high. A babe might be tied onto their backs as well. They wore the traditional cotton garment, the lapa, hand-stamped in dark ink. The fabric tied like a sarong, exposing beautiful bare breasts. There was no self-consciousness, these women were as regal as they were visual, walking the avenues with a slow and serene pace. I was astounded by how much weight they piled on top of their heads. My impression is still of dark-skinned men, some quite short, others tall and angular, but the women were all eight-foot-tall goddesses.

Accra was a bustling city, bursting with busy markets and hand-dyed fabrics. Fruits and vegetables spilled from a sprawl of handmade baskets, brightly colored. Everywhere grew canna and hibiscus and giant scarlet and gold-striped croton plants, hues supersaturated by the dazzling sun. Street sellers offered masks, fertility images, and carved ebony; there was little ivory but much gold. Gold and brass trinkets were sold on the streets here like New York vendors sold hot dogs and falafel. The city was recently built in an airy white scrolled style, reminiscent of the ancient European fortresses that dotted the shore. Slavers had used those fortresses, a use at odds with the sunny serenity of the place and the people. The forts were large, imposing, decaying white structures, originally built by the Portuguese, later used by the Dutch, the English, and other colonial powers. Crew members were drawn to visit them, but I could not. They stank of screams and brutality and despair, their auras muddy and stagnant. Turning my back left me facing sunlit Ghana again, the smiling gentle people, the Ashanti culture of kings and kente cloth, goddesses and gold, felicity and fertility.

Our hotel was a massive white structure with huge geyser-like fountains. It had no real air conditioning and at night I would listen to the drums call through the open windows until sleep finally stole me away. By day we played, the first day in the surf. This was a far different Atlantic than the one I knew. There were sandy beaches, but the sand ended at the shore. Below the water was red sandstone, carved by wave action into a myriad of deep gullies and trenches underfoot. It was extremely treacherous, the gullies sharp with trapped shells, knocked into razor-edged fragments by the raging surf. Anemones and spiky sea creatures were awash in the trenches as well. The swells pounded the shore with relentless ferocity, swirling and smashing. I frolicked in the water with my roommate Sheri and a flight engineer. The ferocious undertow forced us often into a crouch to fight it. I held my own in slightly deeper water, getting into the exotic locale of sun and surf, lulled by our nearness to shore. I looked to anchor myself in the pounding surf on a large boulder, ten feet tall, nearby and somehow moving in the sunlight. A closer look revealed a forest of menacing black crabs waving their large pincers in the sun. Hundreds of huge black crabs, insidiously demonstrating their malicious intent! Thoughts of Stanley and Livingston in my brain, I fought my way out of the surf, falling, getting pounded, scraping my knees, stepping on spiny creatures, cutting my feet. This was Africa, goddamn it, not a splash in a kiddie pool! Remember the bug that ate Livingstone's ear?

Later, those who watched from the window of the nearby yacht club told of their amazement that we would risk such a notoriously dangerous undertow and the fierce waves. Caution from apprehensive observers standing at a window was easily dismissed. I had prevailed in far more challenging circumstances; I was as a veteran of the Peshawar Road. These watchers had their fear of the unknown, and some also had unfortunate prejudices. Like many westerners confronted with cross-culturalism, they compared all they saw to what they knew. Locked in the confines of their limited perceptions, many missed the real Africa.

Everywhere juju charms hung from bushes. There were churches, and a large Muslim presence, but tribal beliefs held sway. The tribes were a blend of Ashanti, Dagomba, and Ga. A nascent national Ghanian identity could also be discerned. Most fantastic were the signs, in English, for the various trades. They were posted on every home, handwritten advertisements. A person's name would be given, with specialties listed underneath, such as "brain surgery and wart removal" or "stomach medicine and dreams explained." The signs are probably gone now, but I hope some anthropologist somewhere has archived the incredible cultural transition that they were a marker of.

The drums took over the night, every night. Crowds would gather by the riverbank near the hotel, and soon the men would send their rhythms across the hills and savannahs into the bush. Their talk would be answered by others somewhere deeper in the bush. Many drums would speak, and if one listened long enough, more voices would be heard cross talking the language of the drum. One to another, the rhythms changing; slowing, elongating, accenting different parts of the beat, the talk vibrated between the local speakers and the distant ones. I was able to discern patterns, questions or statements sent out by the men on the riverbanks, answers coming back across the veld. Sometimes the local drums went silent, and we listened to the drum cross talk deeper in the bush.

The women threw themselves into the angular movements of the dance with joyful abandon. I listened in the throbbing darkness and marveled. Words like strength and power and universality came to mind, and the gladness of the human spirit in its celebration of earth and fire, sky and sea, passion and fertility. I am much older now; I have a first-born son who stands with the straight back of the men of the djembe and talks the talk of the drum with his hands. He got his first gig with a dance company at the age of fourteen. I like to think that the talking drums of West Africa on those long hot nights vibrated the matrices of my DNA and that translated down to him, along with a warrior spirit. We know that the heart entrains to the drum, synchronizes its beat with the bigger beat going on around it. Perhaps histones can do that as well, and this is the secret power of epigenetics, nurture v. nature, leading to novel gene expression reflecting the resonance of experience. On an atomic level, it's all vibration anyway.

In the midst of this midnight madness, with passion thrumming the very air, was it any wonder that what came next was love? The profound mystery itself; I was swept away in the silver sea under a full October moon hanging above the equatorial sky. Running before the currents, it was magical, treacherous and deep. He was tall, blue-eyed and blonde, and quietly powerful in his laid-back way. We went into the bush for our first date, drinking palm wine, villagers calling out their welcomes. There were ebony men swathed in bright and black cloth with walking sticks and an angular, predators' gait. Dead jungle cats hung staked by pathways, tongues protruding clotted blood from open, well-fanged mouths. The villagers let me photograph them, hooting and hollering, making faces. Some women wore bits of western clothing, but the men were still dressed in traditional garb. Walking the shore of the Gold Coast, Rick collected shells while I tried to photograph the shadows of the palm fronds on the sand, ever elusive in the wind. I felt caressed by the soft sea breeze. Sand crabs the size of my fist popped vertically to the surface, no one but I sat on a blanket on the beach. Rick preferred the verandah of a little hut under the palms. He would not allow photographs, because he had to fly later, he said, and it might affect his luck.

The Ghanian air force, pilots for the national airline, had been trained in the USSR by the Soviets. Poorly trained, unfortunately. The government had to lease American pilots to captain the aircraft and give the Ghanians on the job training. They served as co-pilots, flying mostly DC-8's and learning from the Americans as they went. The lure for American fliers was not just a paycheck, it was the call of the frontier. Air traffic control did not regulate the airspace here, radio range was very limited. Once takeoff was achieved, you could hot rod, at an altitude and airspeed of your own choosing. The guys loved the freedom of the skies, and told endless hilarious stories of the ineptness of the Russian-trained flyers. Rick told how he flew home to me, gunning it at seven hundred miles an hour. I was staying at his spacious colonial home by then, with a cook and other household staff. It was all so easy.

The pilots had formed a social enclave with the local embassy personnel in which we were included; there were beach clubs and night spots and rented private villas outside of the city. Ghana Airways had a twice a week run to Europe, the guys flew back planeloads of fresh veggies and eleven-dollar magnums of Dom Perignon. It was a lush and satisfying short-term life. Beach club by day, gold belly chains and bikinis; Rick every night. I didn't have to work, I was a reserve. No one wanted to miss their flights to Saudi Arabia, to the souks and gold markets and the sheiks who gave blonde flight attendants diamond and gold pendants just for having dinner with them.

Rick's uniform included polyester pants, otherwise, he wore cotton. Every pair of pants he owned except the polyester were bleached out in a blazing "V" above the crotch. Every single pair, without exception. I pondered the mystical significance of that. His friend, Captain Joe, said with a wink, "He's got one that lights up." Indeed, he lit up my nights. I felt like the only woman in Ghana. It was just for a month, though. We were going home to November in New York. My heart clutched at the thought. I wasn't experienced enough then to know it was the place and the moment, not just the man. I was head over heels, gone in Ghana.

# Global

Chapter

# 18

# SANDS OF THE SAHARA

Flying north across the Sahara, I lost myself in the view of the shifting sands. It seemed that the vast white world began immediately. It went on for hours, and this time I couldn't spot any caravans inching across the desert. Oases were visible, little clusters of date palms casting their black shadows on the burning sands. They were infrequent, but I was patient, and used to gazing at features of the earth's surface for hours on end. At that time in my life, I was flying the Atlantic at least twice a week.

Sometimes, over the northern part of that ocean, I would fix my gaze on the shifting featurelessness of the water and be rewarded by the sight of icebergs, bobbing cold and transparent on the surface of the deeps. Here, the sand ocean gave rare glimpses of vegetation, the only intimations of life in the vast barrenness. The Sahara cycles between subtropical jungle and arid waste along with the earth's precessional wobble every 23,000 years. Eons before, the Tethys Sea, linking the Atlantic and Pacific oceans, covered what are now those boundless scorching sands. Skeletons of whales and crocodiles lie under the parched Sahara. I doubted that life was as abundant in the burning heat of the last few thousand years as it once was below the surface of the ancient teeming seas. What was exceptional was that humanity had made no mark on the endless sands below, just as traces of the human race were invisible far out over the ocean deeps and the volcanic ice fields of Greenland. The planet primeval, untouched by humanity's hordes, the visuals a rare gift for a keen-sighted human flying in a silver bird at 35,000 feet. "The oceans heaved, the blowing sand scorched, and ice mountains towered in their freedom and wildness…" [18]

Rocks began to appear, and the pristine whiteness took on an orange glow. In a few air moments the unending white sand desert had morphed into a panorama of red rock, a stunning transformation. The rock seemed to become redder and more convoluted as we flew ever northward. Spires and twists curled below, chimneys and gullies and plateaus. Mali had long since given way to Algeria. Then the rock piles rose to be mountains, the Atlas range, which stretch east across Morocco to all the way to Libya. I was studying their convolutions eagerly, excited by the change, when suddenly, shockingly, deep blue water appeared at the very edge of the red rock shelf.

It was a huge, vivid, cobalt blue sea. With a jolt I realized that we were over the Mediterranean.

Northward we flew, on to the Bundes Republik of Deutschland. We would lay over in Munich before heading back to New York in autumn. I stopped window gazing at that point. Africa was gone and so was Rick, the visible change in terrain making me all too conscious of my loss. I knew it was done. Returning to a dark and cold New York winter was a bleak prospect.

We landed in Munich in the midst of Oktoberfest. Big blond men in lederhosen walked the streets, apple cheeked and smiling. Some carried yards of beer, undoubtedly in metric equivalents. Their fraus were equally jolly, enjoying their holiday. There were huge tents set up all over the city, every hotel was crammed with revelers. The beer halls vibrated with song and steins smashing down on tabletops to their refrains until dawn. Oktoberfest is a two-week long celebration of beer and *gemütlichkeit*—the Deutsch concept of cordiality. The festival draws millions, all intent on a good time. The crew joined in, thrilled to have landed in the middle of Germany's oldest and biggest party.

By day, I did my usual routine in a Deutsch city, headed to the market for dark rye bread, hazelnusse spread, and apfelsaft, exchanging greetings with the grocer in German. The food was reassuringly familiar but tasted like ashes. I sat by the large window of my hotel room, looking out into the grayness. The air was wet, low-lying cloud cover, the contrast to the wide-open blue skies of Africa overwhelmed me. I felt hemmed in by the very sky. I gazed down to the street scene, fifteen floors below. Bright green and blue cars, which the Germans called "ducks," careened around cobblestone corners. Police vehicles with sharp sirens screamed by with flashing lights. The traffic was relentless, colors too bright and artificial even in the muted light of a rain-soaked afternoon. I longed for Africa.

Lying in bed high above the city in the predawn darkness, smatterings of songs intruded through the open windows. Militant groups of young Neo-Nazis marched through the streets at night, robotically intoning their chants to the glories of Germany's failed fascist dreams. Orders for home never came. I swam in the hotel pool, haunted the markets, and contemplated love, loss, and the approaching winter in New York. My first inkling of radical change was when I returned to the hotel to find a group of pilots gathered in a hallway, yelling and gesturing. Wondering why they were so animated, I sidled closer to hear their conversation. An aircraft had been ordered back to Africa!

Crews were streaming in from Kano and Lagos in Nigeria to join the Accra contingent that I was part of. I had run into people who I hadn't even known were on Hajj. We all speculated about return orders. The when the word came down, it was all about seniority, the most junior people on the lists were going back. And that, almost certainly, meant me. My first year of flying, at the bottom of the list, getting to go on Hajj twice!! Those who loved the Hajj were enthusiastic, but after four weeks in the equatorial heat and humidity, even the most ardent adventurers were wilted and ready to pack it in. Not me! I sent a telegram to Rick informing him that I would be in Lagos, a place he flew into twice a week. Only Togo and Benin would lay between us and a reuptake of romance. Back to the sun!

This time, I just might get across the Red Sea to the sands of Saudi Arabia and help the Hajjis to their holy ground.

# Global

Chapter

# 19

☷

# HIJACK ON THE TARMAC/
# LAND OF THE IBO

M utiny was in the air. Married men and women were missing their families, others were simply too far away from the familiar for far too long. After five weeks on the road, instead of heading back to New York dapped golden and rust by autumn, twenty-three people had to cross the burning white ocean of Sahara again. Those heading out of Nigeria spoke in heavy tones of warning, "Don't even brush your teeth with the water, eat nothing unless it comes out of a can." They had never seen the squatters of Afghanistan, or the staggering blind of Pakistan, or the savage sadhus at the Red Fort in Delhi. Had they ever picked cooked flies out of their curry or lived on mystery mush and sheep shit tea? This whole foods vegan happily accepted canned ravioli and chemical concoctions from those heading back to the happy place of the USA. Canned food was the way to go now.

A new crew, assembled from the junior folk lowest in seniority, prepared for take-off across the Sahara. Our task was to evacuate thousands of Mecca-bound pilgrims who had been stranded on a little airstrip in Nigeria. How many Lagos-Jeddah airport trips we would actually fly was yet to be determined. We had room for 252 souls, and if we flew out immediately after getting our legal rest, we might get most of them on the Saudi Arabian peninsula before the moon was full. At the full of the moon, the Hajjis had to have completed their stations of approach and be at the altar in Mecca.

The charming Captain Jack was our commander-in chief. A bright and funny fellow, Jack had asked me months before to bid the Hajj and be his playmate in Africa. Flying with him was always entertaining, full of hilarity and pranks. He had a new wife, a small child, and 25 years on me. There was no way it was going to happen, but I did enjoy his company. The crew also included two blonde babes from Long Island who had done Ghana with me. We liked to run around in bikinis once the passengers had deplaned. Spirits were high as we headed out over the Sahara again. Little did we know we were flying into the most extreme turbulence we would ever experience – on the ground.

Our route was slightly eastward of our previous trans-Sahara flight paths. Over southern Algeria, dark masses of mountains began to appear. It was the Ahaggar range, defunct volcanic monoliths thrusting dramatically above a dark granite plateau. The Ahaggar are a huge rock island set in the Saharan sands, some of which reach nearly 10,000 feet. The mountain range is about the size of France, and indeed the French have a dark history there. A large expedition was sent south in 1881 to reconnoiter the route for a proposed French-built railway to traverse the Sahara. They were massacred to a man by the Ahaggar tribesmen, the Tuareg, armed only with medieval weapons. Translated from the Arabic, Tuareg means "abandoned of God." This fierce desert tribe converted late to Islam, and their sword-wielding men take the veil at puberty, covering their faces to protect against inhaling evil spirits through their mouths. The unveiled women were known to dominate the family units. They were not fond of strangers.

We were out over the western flank of the Ahaggar range, over the Tenezrouft, the "land of thirst." This was the place where caravans had traditionally abandoned their malcontents, leaving them to bleach to bare bones. Without aid from the Tuareg, there was no escape from the Tenezrouft but death. We were having engine trouble, yet again. Number four had conked out, two was badly leaking oil. There was no landing strip anywhere nearby. The company needed us to get to Lagos and make good on important contracts. I practiced "Ana dheef Allah" (I am a guest of God). Guest right is a sacred duty in Islam. If worst came to worst, I have always had a fondness for a man with a bare chest and a sword. Allah hu Akbar.

Cap'n Jack had his eyes on the sky and his hands on the wheel. He valiantly sailed our ship over those extinct and forbidding monoliths reaching so malevolently for the sky. On my journeys through the heartlands of Islam, I had often memorized local sayings that might be identify me as more than a tourist. It was an anthropological tool and forced a connection between the person of indigenous culture and the foreigner who might be trespassing on cultural mores. I had no qualms about using Arabic phrases. Eastern philosophy teaches that all paths lead to the same place, that there are common universal truths underlying all religions. One could embrace tenets of Islam, Judaism, Christianity, Buddhism, Taoism, and Hinduism without cognitive dissonance. Undoubted heresy to the orthodox, but the weave of common threads unites us all.

A plane had been dropped at an airport with only one airstrip, incoming or outbound. Thousands of Hajjis had been grounded for eight days while the aircraft was scraped off the tarmac. The Hajjis were sweltering on the asphalt by day and by night, they were watching the moon wax bigger in the sky. At the full of the moon, they had to have completed their rituals on the plain of Arafat and be present at the Ka'aba, the altar in Mecca. Thousands of miles away, food and water running low, they waited. The dream of their lifetime was tick, tick, ticking away. We were the first plane in.

Even before we stopped engines, we were surrounded by a living stream of humanity. I opened the aircraft door. Ah, Africa, the wind like a furnace of fragrant flora and spice. We were greeted by the sight of a rich panoply of pilgrims and African tribesmen, each group in their native dress and headgear, each with a distinctive body language of rage. There were tall and angular ebony men in orange and black robes, all with seven-foot staffs that they pounded menacingly upon the ground. There were café-au-lait almond-eyed men in blue caftans and the burgundy fez, their tassels shaking with the stomping of their feet. There were legions of short round men, dressed in red and gold batik, grunting and pushing as one mass. Bigger men in green djellabas with bold black stripes pounded their chests as one being. One of the crew began taking photos, a directly prohibited action. Fists pumped the air as this mass of humanity seethed toward us. When the fists came up, I immediately backed away from the open door. Running into the cockpit, there was Jack on the radio, yelling to the tower "We want guns! We want guns!"

The screaming furor of thousands beat at us in waves. I spied a portable stairway in the distance, and my heart sank. It was only a matter of time until the crowd realized that they could push it to the aircraft and storm us. We would be hostages, a daunting prospect. Heads turned toward the stairway and I witnessed the idea ignite as one mind. The frenzy was so great that those in front resisted the push of those at the back who were fighting to get the stairway to the plane. It bought us time. I ran back to tell Jack, who was still barking on the tower frequency. From the cockpit windows, I suddenly saw dozens of little men dressed in pith helmets and Bermuda shorts spilling out of the terminal, tweeting mightily on whistles! It looked like a 1940s movie set of where the locals called the Brits "Bwana." They began dragging away rioters from under the aircraft, and the captain somehow managed to fire the engines. The noise was deafening, the doors were still open!

The rioters were ready. Dying on the way to Mecca was believed by many in Islam to be a blessing for the pilgrim, assuring the cleansing of sins and admission to heaven. The would-be martyrs lay down in front of the aircraft with transfixed looks of beatific happiness on their faces. Some opened their arms, some looked up at the sky, all smiled serenely, transported in bliss at the prospect of their imminent deaths. Tweet! Tweet! The airport security forces stormed into the uproar, dragging the Paradise-bound bodily from beneath the fuselage. Most of the crowd was broadside to the aircraft, and now heavily involved in making a human corridor for the stairway to access the plane.

Jack saw an opening and went for it. He raced the aircraft down the taxiway like a defensive end with a football, hell-bent on a touchdown. He zigged and zagged and curved and made a series of evasive maneuvers, turns designed to camouflage our passage deeper and deeper into the bowels of the freight area of the airport. The crew held onto the seat backs for dear life as unaccustomed wind and deafening noise roared through the open cabin. This time when Jack cut engines, heavily armed Nigerian military were at the portable stairs, guns at the ready. We were hustled off into waiting limos and pushed down on the floor. The soldiers crouched, their automatic weapons blazing in all directions. The drivers gunned it and the airport was left behind in the dust. I sat up to see where in the world I was.

The streets of the topical city of Lagos were crowded, noisy, and unbelievably polluted. The rusting vans that were used as local buses belched black fumes heavily into the air. The smell of exhaust reeked, and every engine in the capital city knocked and sputtered and spewed. It was a nightmare. The heat and humidity were intolerable combined with the choking fumes and the crowds. Everywhere people tried to jump onto the vans, falling and getting flattened. Those in possession of space made no room to accommodate the would-be hangers on. I had seen people fall on their faces before, in Asia, trying to jump on to a moving vehicle. It made the New York City subways look like cow pasture, blissful bovines placidly chewing their cud. The press of humanity made it seem hotter, there was no ambiance of serene gentility as there had been in Ghana, no smiling faces.

The Ibo of eastern Nigeria were a fierce warrior race. Women of the Ibo and Fulani shared combat duty alongside their men in the 19th century. In the 20th century most Ibo were Christian, primarily Catholics. The Hausa-Fulani of the northern region were Muslim. Together with the Yoruba of the west, now largely Protestant, these diverse ethnic groups were lumped together into a country called Nigeria by the British. It is a basic tenet of imperialism to deny the cultural identities of conquered groups and to focus instead on their differences from the ruling class. Thus, Nigeria was created as a country of Africans, disregarding those peoples' unique cultural and ethnic identities. This same recipe was used in creating Afghanistan and countries of the Middle East, and its short-sightedness still boggles the thinking mind. Independence from Britain came late to Nigeria, in 1960, and only five years later the country was embroiled in severe crisis, with a poorly trained military seriously divided by ethnic factionalism attempting to take control of the government.

The discovery of oil in the late 1950's had changed the economy from subsistence agrarian-based one to that of a major petroleum exporter blessed with low-sulfur crude. Rapid industrialization began, but there were no deeply rooted national values to act as a nucleus upon which to build a shared Nigerian identity. Regional infighting raged between the newly Christian-educated Ibo of the east and the Muslims of the north, who themselves had little ethnic unity beside their Islamic religion. The Yoruba fought fiercely against the northern Muslims; as a well-centralized economic and political group, they had advantage over the fiercely individualistic and historically chieftain less Ibo. These tensions led to a military coup in 1966 and erupted in civil war a year later. Then the eastern Ibo seceded from Nigeria to form Biafra. The resultant war killed more than a million people in three years. Assassinations, more military coups, and regional strife continued for years. The debacle of foreign oil interests raping the resources, degrading the environment, and destroying traditional methods of livelihood added fuel to the raging fires.

Lagos was no stranger to rioting and bloodshed, the urban areas of this most populous nation in Africa had been swamped by an influx of rural immigrants seeking the advantages of city life. Lagos Colony had been a scene of strife and shredded by war. We deplaned in Lagos just a year after the latest coup. Military rule held the city in a tight and tense grip. Transported to the hotel in groups of twos and threes, we fell on each other in the lobby, adrenalin still pumping, yelling and screaming our stories at each other to process the pandemonium that we had been hostage to. Overly excited, shouting, trembling, some swilling from little silver flasks, we unwittingly set the stage for another debacle. Hotel reception stared at us with total hostility. At first, the sullen state of the occupants of the hotel lobby was an oddity of little importance. We were totally oblivious, reliving the riot, caught up in the emotional aftermath of our narrow escape from being stormed and hijacked. Finally, the strained severity of the situation dawned on us, and we realized that the attitude was seriously amiss. What was up? Our pilots, several of them ex-military officers, took command of the situation. The soldiers with their guns had gone back for our luggage and then vanished, no officials were present to smooth our way. Eventually, after much negotiation, successful pressure was put upon the staff and they began to give out rooms, but they took their sweet time. Narrowed eyes, frowning faces, resistance and outright rudeness were the order of the day.

Twenty-three white-assed people headed somberly toward their rooms. The hotel was cavernous. Its corridors went on for city blocks, dirty and dim. There was no electricity. Candles were the sole source of illumination, dripping wax and runneling on the floors. Porters in native dress peopled the corridors, hunkered down on their haunches, blatantly assessing our assets. The bane of the flight attendant, to have to share a room when hotels were crowded, seemed a blessing here. We were housed in a dead-end hallway, far from the lobby. I was eager to get in the hotel room, to shower, to wash off the sweat and stickiness of stress. Pushing the door open, I thought I felt the slight stir of a breeze. Could there be air conditioning? Not likely, with no power. There were two beds, the sheets looked clean, and that was the sum of the amenities. The bathroom had not seen running water in years. The taps were open, rusted and ruined. Tub, sink, and toilet were stained and brown with oxidation and disuse. Filth and dust were everywhere. My roommate was exclaiming about the marks on the carpet, she went silent with shock when I showed her the bathroom.

We locked the door and piled tables and chairs against it. There were no cell phones or then, code knocks and telephone rings had to be arranged with the other crew. I thought that there was a real chance that we would have need of each other. My roommate promptly laid down and passed into an exhausted sleep. Pacing and restless, I could not possibly relax. Opening the room's only window flooded it with noxious vapors. The coughing engines of the buses reverberated loudly, belching fumes, there was no music in the cacophony of this city's streets. I thought of Accra, and Rick, and how the rhythms of the drums there had entrained my heart and stolen me softly to sleep at night. How very far I was from Rick and Ghana, fair Afrique. I wept.

Tomorrow dawned another day. The Muslim north was beckoning, there was talk of moving the crews up to Kano for a base as the standards at this hotel were unacceptable. Kano was a most interesting place, deep in the interior, with a homogenized local populace. Using no right angles, stunning circular shapes dominated the architecture of their homes and mosques. Even their colors were soothing, the terracottas and earthy oranges and burnt siennas reminiscent of southern Italy. One could experience pastoral Africa instead of the frictions of a tumultuous multi-ethnic port city. My dormant anthropologist genes started encoding hope, soon to be dashed. Despite the scene at our arrival, the rest of our lively international crew were not dismayed by Lagos. They preferred the ambiance of urban port chaos to a dry (non-alcohol) and sedate religious environment. The tropical skies were a rich blue, and we decided that a new day deserved a new beginning. We headed out into the hot and savory breeze for another glimpse of Africa, in a group of about ten.

We toured the markets on foot. They smelled of fish and spice and exhaust and human sweat. Brightly dyed clothing and batik hung from wash lines and hand-cranked sewing machines were everywhere. There were some hostile glances, but mostly we encountered indifference. We were stopped by a stranger for the first time about a half a mile from the hotel. In English, she told us to go back, that we were not safe walking the streets. By consensus, we walked on. Later, near the waterfront, we became aware that the hustle and bustle of activity had gone silent. People had stopped what they were doing and stood staring. Not a single face was friendly. Every move we made was watched by a gathering and increasingly hostile crowd. Suddenly uncertain, we stood in an uneasy grouping, deciding what to do. A couple approached and told us that we were in extreme danger and must leave, immediately. This time the threat was palpable, imminent. Turning as a unit, we beat feet. Intense scrutiny followed us all the way back to the hotel, targets of whispers, resentment, and impending malevolence. Hearts were pounding, danger acrid in the air. Heads down, we retraced our steps in silence and speed. Even the pilots were mute. At the hotel, we were informed of the murder of foreign tourists by a hostile mob just a few days before.

There was nowhere to go, no real place to feel safe except gathered together in one of the rooms. We huddled there by day, telling stories and playing cards. Except for a few hours in the afternoon, there was no electricity. Food was another problem; detailed diarrhea reports came in from those who had braved the hotel restaurant. Afghani poisons still rumbling in my gut, there was no way that I was subjecting myself to enteric pathogens again. My store of canned food was running low and most of the time I was hungry, the walls of my empty stomach seemingly rubbing against each other. Washing was a real dilemma. Bottled water was not yet available, we had arrived with canteens of tap water which we purified with chlorine. This was used for tooth brushing and the barest of face dampening. Since there was no running water and none to buy, our canteens had to last for the duration, and no one knew how long that would be. And it was hot, hot, hot.

The hotel had a swimming pool. Larger than Olympic size, it dwarfed the outdoor veranda. There was no filtration and the pool had not seen chlorine in years. It was used as a communal bathtub. At any given time, there would be dozens of local people in the pool, shampooing their hair, lathering with soap, splashing and playing in the gray slime. The hotel guests sat frozen on deck chairs, completely unnerved. I went there only once. Broiling in the equatorial sunshine and not being able to swim was utterly unbearable to me. Growing up on my parents' boat on Long Island, I had been surrounded by the sea. The product of thousands of seashore afternoons, the seduction of was water irresistible to me. Sauntering into the pool, wading to just above my knees, the liquid was opaque, gray. I was dying for coolness, my hands went in. A pungent smell, stagnation and brewing microbes, went up my nostrils as the cupped hot water neared my face. I dropped it like a person scalded and beat it out of the pool. The hot sun shone down on me, dispirited and sweating.

The power came on in the afternoons and with it, the television came to life. There was only one TV station, broadcasting in black and white. The language was English. Raised eyebrows, intimidation, and threats were the order of the day. The programs all touted the policies of the regime, lauded its efforts on behalf of the citizens, and threatened severe repercussions for non-compliance with party policy. The most amazing was "The Nightly News with Bimbo Roberts." This large and intimidating lady had her own daily news show. It opened with a shot of her grim countenance, turbaned and caftaned, her eyes boring into the camera. She intoned warnings about the nefarious and illegal activities that various citizens had been found guilty of that day. Threatening "you know who you are, and we do too," Bimbo promised swift retribution for all misdeeds while the camera panned to downtrodden citizens being handcuffed and led away in dejection. It wasn't Big Brother, it was Big Momma, fat, fascist, and a mouthpiece for the regime! The international news, such as it was, placed all events in a pro or anti-Nigeria context. It reminded me of Galileo and the medieval Catholic church. The sun had to spin around the earth, there was no other point of view admitted. If you did not conform to the government's current mouthspeak, you were in danger, and eyes and ears were everywhere.

I never missed an opportunity to watch Bimbo's latest imprecations, she was fascinating. I spent the afternoons in the room of Susan and Richard, the "Flying Baldwins," playing cards and watching their TV. It was crew camaraderie, inspired by the graciousness of the Baldwins and our determination to make the best of a challenging situation. All too soon, however, I was a prisoner in my hotel room. My friends would jaunt off to Saudi Arabia, flying across the Red Sea. They returned with stories of the Hajjis' singing and devotion, and dripping gold from the souks. I was a reserve, and not needed unless someone was ill. As no one wanted to be left behind, sitting unwashed in the stifling hotel room with little food or water all day long, my services were not in demand.

Finally, and thankfully, a check stew showed up. I was due for an observation, she had orders for my departure to Jeddah airport, twelve miles down the road from Mecca. I was outta there.

Chapter

# 20

☷

# A STAIRWAY IN SAUDI ARABIA

The Hajjis prayed five times a day, in the direction of Mecca. Our captain thought they were bowing to the plane and didn't realize that the aircraft was between the devout and their holy city. Gone was the unique dress of the individual tribes, the Hajjis wore the white attire of the pilgrim. The men carried little metal pots, like the small aluminum ones found in scout kits. Muslims practice extreme cleanliness and are required to use water to wash after toileting, these little pots seemed to be assisting their personal hygiene.

There were animals on board, to be slaughtered in remembrance of Ibrahim's willingness to sacrifice his only son in obedience to divine will. Men milled about, refusing to take their seats, blocking the aisles and forestalling safety measures. They ignored the orders of the mostly female cabin crew, although we were uniformed. It was

1977, these were rural twentieth century Africans, unfamiliar with technology, safety procedures, or gender equality. The plane couldn't taxi until the passengers were seated and belted in. I began reaching into men's robes to find seatbelts, startling many. I wordlessly fastened and tightened dozens of them, in closer physical proximity than I wanted to be to a population with running eye diseases and other conditions underexposed to medical care.

Most passengers did not know how to unfasten their seat belts, which kept them restrained while we dealt with others, unfamiliar with aircraft, who were urinating on the emergency chutes. Once someone caught on to undoing their seatbelt, everyone else got it quickly, of course, foiling our plan. No one among us spoke Arabic or any African languages. We were unaccustomed to passengers who were completely indifferent to our authority. I did the best I could with the seatbelts, the senior flight attendant ran to the cockpit with her woes and finally, we just took off.

On most Hajj flights, the pilgrims sang songs of devotion and piety. This group went silent, some reading the Qu'ran, most very contemplative. There were ululations, rocking the silence of our droning through the sky. Many had already donned the white garb of Ihram, holy preparation for their impending devotions. Performing the Hajj is required at least once in a lifetime for all Muslims who are financially and physically able. It is one of the five pillars of Islam and brings together the largest gathering of humans for any purpose on the planet. Millions of pilgrims from all over the world unite for the purpose of spiritual odyssey. The tasks required in performing the Hajj were many and have been modified over the decades due to crowd size and safety concerns. On the first day, a day of prayer, the intention to perform the Hajj was reaffirmed, and the restrictions of Ihram were embraced, including the bearing of no weapons, no wanton destruction of animal or plant life, and sexual abstention. Day two brought a journey to the barren plain of Arafat, where the seekers stood vigil for the day, atoning and repenting of their sins and seeking the mercy of Allah. That night was spent in prayer under an open sky, and pebbles were gathered for the ritual stoning of Shaitan, the Devil, on the third day. Pilgrims climbed a bridge to cast their seven stones at the largest of three pillars which symbolize Satan. Once that ritual act was completed, the sacrificial animals were slaughtered, and the festival of Eid al Adha began elsewhere in the Islamic world. Male pilgrims shaved their heads and the women trimmed the dead ends off their hair. This event-filled day finished with a Tawaf (circumambulation) around the Ka'aba, demonstrating love and obedience to God. The holy Ka'aba, which resembles an extraterrestrial black stone cube, is thought to originate from the archangel Gabriel. On days four and five, the Hajjis again stoned the three pillars of Shaitan. The final Tawaf was performed on the sixth or sometimes the seventh day, as the Hajjis circumambulated the stone seven times in a counterclockwise direction in a ritual of farewell. Kissing the Ka'aba was required until recently, but the size of crowds has loosened this requirement for physical contact.

After a few hours of flying, the desert was done and we were over the vast Red Sea. Gazing on its sparkling blueness, waves tossing in the sunlight, I tried unsuccessfully to picture it parting for Moses. We landed, and the pilgrims deplaned, disappearing into the desert with gravity and a somber elegance. We were not allowed to get off for the aircraft, not able to visit the souks and famed gold markets of Saudia. Mecca itself was twelve miles away, our foreign presence near the holy city at this significant time was unacceptable. There were no parties or fancy dinners, it was nearly a full moon over Mecca, and even the most Westernized of the sheiks were immersed in their piety.

My friends Cors and Smitty were on board, and went into action once the length of our holdover became known. They stripped down to bikinis, decorated the aircraft with streamers made from plastic tray liners, and turned up the music, loud. It was dance party time! We were an oasis unto ourselves, commanders of our own ship set on the edge of a vast killing desert, where even as we partied, women were in recovery from clitorectomies. When the slow songs came on, I shed some tears thinking of Rick. Ghana Airways had a trip into Lagos, everyone had expected me to go out to the terminal and meet the flight. I didn't see the point. He knew I was in Lagos; he could have found me if he tried. He didn't. The loud speakers boomed the classic bar song, "You Are So Beautiful to Me."[19] Guess not.

Seeking solitude, I sat outside on the portable stairs, looking over the desert, distorted by heat mirage. It was endlessly flat and monochromatic, not one whit of color or variance in topography. The whiteness was blinding on the ground, brighter seeming than even the Sahara. I could smell only dust and sand. Oil rigs marred the landscape, metal monsters chomping for crude. There wasn't a human in sight. Saudia, ruled by a royal dynasty, restricted women's rights, mobility, and sexuality. Women couldn't even drive in this country, or be seen outside alone. I gazed around me, uneasy.

Before leaving New York, I had heard news which had rocked my world. My close friend Nancy, a dancer, was pregnant. She was a sister of the soul; we had spent long winters by the fireside, warmed by our friendship and the flames. We shared our perspectives, our dreams, and our hopes for the future, which included children. Both of us were involved with artists, driven creative types who loved from a distance, centered in themselves, never committing to any relationship above the one they had with their art. In our late twenties, our biological clocks ticking, we were secretly yearning for that most consummate of relationships, motherhood. We didn't readily admit this, it was the 1970s, when women were exploring liberation from the traditional expectations of patriarchal society. It would take the actuality of giving birth to realize that producing another human being is the ultimate creative act.

My friend had stepped into the mystery, crossed over into that long-desired place, changed her life, forever. As she had done it, could it be far behind for me? I had left my jazz musicians. The aviator had stolen my heart, but dropped the ball. What was next? How could I manifest becoming a mother and still explore my fascinations? What kind of career would allow a single parent the time to anchor a new life while providing adequate financial support? Certainly not the one I was in. This was not the first time that I had contemplated raising a child alone. A marriage would be a better choice, but was far from certain in my future.

There was much to ponder, sitting on that stairway, surrounded by stillness and the shifting sands of Saudi Arabia.

Chapter

# 21

☰

# EXIT AFRICA, IN DARKNESS

The Hajj was over for this year, the moon past full, rituals completed, blessings earned. We were finally going home. All of the Hajjis who could be airlifted before the full moon had been flown in. They had deplaned with their little pots and bundles and sacrificial animals, heading towards Mecca without a backward glance. I had been gone almost seven weeks, it felt as long as my year long journey in Asia.

There was one more drama, one more spectacle to unfold. We had to get out alive. We were back in Nigeria, in Lagos, at the same cavernous and dangerous hotel, in the same group of barricaded rooms. Windows were firmly closed against the reeking air pollution and noise. There was still no running water, still no air conditioning, and no food safe to eat. A sponge bath or three on the aircraft had left me much refreshed, at least temporarily.

We all dreamed of immersing our entire bodies in clean, soapy water. Home was tugging on the heartstrings; spouses and kids for many, friends and father for m

The ground agents gave us stern warnings about having our luggage outside our doors by two AM. They returned three times, moving up the deadline and becoming more and more strident in their cautions and admonitions. We had concerns about leaving our belongings in the hallway of this decrepit, rancorous hotel, but the agents were adamant. Eventually, our departure time was moved up to one AM, with the bags spirited away by truck long before then. What could be the reason for this high anxiety?

We waited on the tarmac in the dirty aircraft, grumpy and sleep deprived. The Nigerian night was black as coal. There were no electric lights in evidence except for a dim glow in the distant terminal, lit by its own generator. Those who have never seen a natural night, unspoiled by any reflection or light pollution, will never know the power and mystery of darkness. It is a great, unmourned casualty of modern living.

The ship's officers fussed in the cockpit, closing the door on our eager ears. The copilot, who had the job of filing the flight plan, finally emerged with the flight plan in hand, and disappeared into the terminal. He didn't return for a long while, and I felt the tension of the cockpit crew rise. He came back only briefly and left again, as surreptitiously as possible. All of our inquiries as to the nature of the delay were stonewalled.

It was a long night in the dark predawn, parked on the Nigerian airstrip, awaiting departure clearance. Our sleep had been forfeited in order to sit on the aircraft and wait. The tension and secrecy were palpable. We were used to delays, they were part of the business, but delays were usually explained promptly so that we could keep the passengers informed. This was a ferry flight, there were no passengers, and apparently no explanations either. The co-pilot came racing back to the aircraft, darted into the cockpit, ran out again. I watched him hustle, hurrying back to the terminal. What the hell was going on? The first glimmers of dawn appeared on the horizon. The cockpit went crazy, the captains swearing and pacing in the aisle. I noticed that a sharp lookout was being kept for the copilot. Or perhaps it was the terminal they were watching. The radio was silent.

The cabin crew was becoming very uneasy. Something was terribly wrong. This was an unfriendly country run by a forbidding military regime, hostile to Americans, whites, and foreigners in general. There was enough light to see the taxiway now, just a paved strip in the shadows. Unlike most airports, it had no ground lights to guide take offs or landings. What it did have, however, was considerably more sobering. Huge anti-aircraft guns, portable on wheeled carriages, lined the entire length of the runway. I could see the ammunition belts; the guns were loaded. There were dozens of them, but anyone of them could have done the job.

The captains appeared frantic, the tension at a fever-pitch as the light grew. There was still no sign of the co-pilot. The sky to the east had colored bands, soon the sun would be above the horizon. Our problem was still a mystery, but obviously we needed to be away under the cover of darkness. The large guns pointed in our direction were daunting.

A sudden noise came from the cockpit and the engines roared to life. I saw a man running full tilt, the ground agent. The copilot was behind him, sprinting for all he was worth. No one waited for the customary procedures, there was no leisurely start up while the cabin crew took their seats by the exits and prepared the emergency chutes for take-off. The agent himself slammed the door as soon as the copilot was aboard, four bells (take-off imminent) rang out before we even got to our seats. We were skyward.

The word was not only that we were smuggling, but that our flight plan had been filed under a false name to get us out of the country. It seems that we had contraband on board. We had filed under the name of the national airline, Nigerian Airways. The plan had been for us to be airborne from the darkened airstrip long before the sun came up. As a U.S. carrier, our flag and name were boldly emblazoned on our fuselage. We had been sitting ducks on that runway, surrounded by machine guns, engaged in illegal activities in the middle of a troubled third world country in the grip of a hostile military dictatorship.

We rocketed into the sky, a short, abrupt take-off. I wondered about the guns' range as I watched to see if little soldier stick figures would come running out onto the tarmac. Fortunately, I saw none. I looked out into the dawn with my eagle eyes long after lift-off, glued to the window. The Nigerian air force could intercept a commercial airliner, if they had been scrambled. Would they shoot first, or try to force us down? We had no passengers aboard to complicate matters. The flight droned on and on and on. At last, we cleared Nigerian airspace. Our collective sigh gave us new wings.

# Global

Chapter

# 22

# PEACE COMES TO THE MIDDLE EAST

Cairo was on high alert. Terrorist attacks were expected, even imminent. Arriving a few days later than our reservation, we found soldiers bristling with automatic weapons manning the hotel entrance. They were demanding documents just to get inside to hotel reception. Our date had passed, but I had anticipated little problem as hotels were rarely booked to capacity. What I had not foreseen was the demise of the Shah of Iran and Egypt's agreement to be the site of his funerary rites. The ensuing arrival of scores of diplomats from countries united in honoring the Shah and especially his ally, the USA, had overwhelmed the security forces of Cairo.

It was ironic to be arriving in Egypt when Shah Reza Pahlavi's memorial services were underway. The Shah had been a pariah at his death, rejected and denied sanctuary in other Muslim countries. He had been deposed by the fundamentalist Islamic revolution which brought the Ayatollah Khomeini and his Imams to rule Iran. Pahlavi's pro-Western policies had created a backlash that swept him from power and changed the political climate of the known world. Anwar Sadat, under great pressure from Jimmy Carter, finally allowed Reza Shah to come to Egypt to make his final journey. "Détente" was the buzz word of the moment, Mr. Carter had brought together Egypt and Israel, Muslim and Jew, to the White House Rose Garden to sign historic accords of peace.

The funeral was a high anxiety event because Muslim nations were seeking to dissociate themselves from the past and acknowledge the new power of Khomeini's Islamic fundamentalism. There were serious concerns about which government might fall next to Islamic revolution if it appeared insensitive to the interests of the theocracy. Allies of the United States were under pressure to be respectful to the Shah, a billion-dollar importer of products of the declining U.S. defense industry. The hostage crisis was in full swing, the U.S. embassy in Teheran had been captured by Islamic fundamentalists with an anti-US agenda after the Shah was admitted to an American hospital for cancer treatment.

Although not a primary site for the lodging of diplomats, the Cairo Sheraton, where I had reserved a room, was obviously a possible target for extremist groups. My new husband and I had meandered in the Greek Islands for longer than originally planned. The islands were brimming with disco wannabes in white suits and gold chains, but we had found other delights in the nude beaches and the sun and sea ambiance. We breakfasted al fresco at the harbor where the gulls flew and every other tanned and muscled waiter was named "Adoni" and looked the part. Sun-soaked days were spent lazing on the beaches amidst miscreant donkeys and radiant good will.

And so we were late for the Egyptian portion of the honeymoon, late and ill-timed. After much negotiation, a room at the hotel was finally secured and the honeymoon went on. The Cairo Sheraton was a cool alabaster oasis, exquisitely appointed with marble and carved filigree screens. The sub-Saharan sands reflected the light of the full moon outside our bedroom window. Outside as well were the banks of the legendary Nile. Although in imagination I pictured Cleopatra, the first vessel I saw was not a barge with the painted eye of Horus and a covered platform for a queen. It was singularly arresting though. A tattered a gray sail billowed in the breeze and sent the boat scudding down the river. The backdrop was enormous date palms, with green fronds milling in a light wind on the reddened banks of the Nile.

The river itself was slow and ponderous, curved and sinuous, and smelled of cinnamon and reeds.

As Americans, we were met with smiles and friendly gestures everywhere we went. The cabbies were delighted to convey us and talk about politics. "Jimmy Carter, Jimmy Carter!" they would exclaim happily, as if by transporting Americans, they were personally furthering detente. "Anwar Sadat," we would reply, with mutual delight about the miracle of accord wrought by the peacemaker presidents.

We often passed the City of the Dead while riding around Cairo. An enormous residential graveyard, it is home to extended families in both the nether worlds and this one. The departed were housed in crypts above ground, much like those in New Orleans. While their antebellum counterparts were graced with wrought iron detail and bougainvillea blazing in the sun, these crypts were uniform and colorless externally in the light of day. It was in the darkness that they shone, lit by the flickers of a thousand torches and blazing cook fires. Shadowy figures flitted by, women in black chadors bent on domestic errands. The first time I saw black moving shadows in the City of the Dead, my heart raced and the hairs on the back of my neck rose, I thought I was seeing ghosts. Only after our cabbie explained that thousands of poor inhabited the tombs was I able to appreciate the sounds of children hard at play and the joyful barking of dogs. I always peered into the City, riding by in taxis on tourist missions under the light of sun or moon.

In Cairo, it is a cultural tradition for families to picnic at the site of the dearly departed to do them honor. Many of the larger mausoleums have visiting rooms built within to accommodate overnight guests. The occupation of these graveyards dates from the fourteenth century. Amidst the rectangular monotony of the necropolis were genuine examples of Islamic high architecture. Wealthy families often hired guards to live at the tombs to fend off would-be robbers, and it is said that the air of peace and tranquility around the place encouraged others besides the tomb guardians to move in. The City teems with life; millions of people, many of whom emigrated from rural areas, live within the Dead Zone. It's an anthropologist's fascination. The late twentieth century brought electricity, shops and even schools to the City of the Dead. The necropolis sprawls on the opposite side of Cairo from the wealthy embassy district, on the route to Giza.

The Pyramids of Giza lay on the outskirts of the city, on a plateau on the desert's edge. I was most anxious to experience this sole surviving wonder of the ancient world. The Colossus of Rhodes has fallen, along with the Lighthouse of Alexandria and the Mausoleum at Halicarnassus, all destroyed by earthquakes. The Temple of the fair Artemis and Zeus's likeness are gone, and the Hanging Gardens, both of Babylon and Herat, perfume the air no longer. Khufu's pyramid and the smaller ones stand, not crowned in alabaster limestone as they were in 2500 BCE, but still impressive. There was a light show that night, as there had been at the Parthenon in Greece. We had spent my husband's birthday there, perched on a hill overlooking the ancient ruins, watching the sunset fade as a velvet Athens evening came on. The light show was typical of the era, the whole world was a disco, ludicrous as it was. The show at the Pyramids was in English, this time we got the history as well as the canned drum rolls. The Sahara loomed, abutting the edge of the monuments. A village or two was visible, dimly glimpsed in the sandy distance, and I stood facing southwest with unease in my heart. Ghana was out there, on the south end of that desert, and the ghost of my former self haunted me with her dreams of a different romance. Bedouins on camelback hunkered all around the pyramids, hawking wares for the tourist trade. The scene was tawdry, but they were the real deal, with their turbans and tassels and camel-management skills. We were the only foreigners in sight.

At fifty-six feet, the Pyramids were not tall, smaller than their Mayan counterparts in the jungles of Mexico and Central America. Yet they had been the tallest structures in the known world for almost four thousand years. They were still magestic, set against a backdrop of desert and decorated around their bases with Bedouins on their tasseled camels. We made the pilgrimage route to the Sphinx on horseback. The guardian of the plateau of Giza, the Sphinx or Horus on the Horizon faces due east in homage to the rising sun. A site of solar worship in antiquity, Egyptians made supplication to the Sphinx for the annual flooding of the Nile, upon which their crops depended. Artifacts found suggest other blessings were sought as well. There was a strong sense of presence as I rode my horse towards the lion with the man's face and headdress. I felt like Mary approaching Bethlehem on the back of the donkey.

The Sphinx was alive in the sunset. Its presence was not benevolent, but cryptic and arrogant. I had my own agenda, my own request to lay at the paws of the lion man. I wanted a child, very much, and I had a willing husband. Somehow it was right to address prayers to the entity that was the Sphinx. "Oh, Great Sphinx," I intoned solemnly in the twilight, while my imagination conjured the specter of kneeling obeisances and palm frond fans being waived by sandaled slaves. My entreaties for a child felt magical. Years after my first son was born, I read that, historically, the Sphinx was considered a homing beacon for souls seeking to incarnate on earth. A terrestrial antennae, as it were, emitting a celestial signal. My odd intuition had been culturally on target, and so were my husband's instincts to mount us on horseback for the processional.

Returning to the Pyramids by day, I had uncomfortable feelings about being inside. There was a feeling of oppression. It was clammy within, although it was an intensely hot day, and the smell was strange. I felt short of breath, and the passage was very narrow. Red-faced German tourists were coming down the descending passage, sweating and struggling for air. It was an unexpectedly claustrophobic experience. A guide attached himself to us, a strange little fellow, about five feet tall and nearly as wide. His eyes were blank and cold. He claimed to live in the desert village just beyond the plateau and urged us to venture onto the sands to accompany him to his home. The prospect of such a visit was interesting, but his unsmiling demeanor and urgency did not bode well. We declined. He claimed disappointment to not be bringing Americans to his home to celebrate goodwill and turned the conversation to hidden tombs and crypts.

The evenings brought activity on the streets near the hotel. Veiled women in chadors twittered like birds as they streamed by in large groups, in happy conversation. A cooling breeze off the Nile brought relief from the scorching heat. People thronged by the banks of the river.

Nothing could have prepared me for the Cairo Museum. The Pharaonic relics lay scattered about in piles. Anyone could have walked out of there with armloads of stuff. I was shocked. Growing up in the suburbs of the great city of New York, trips to museums had been regular events. Nothing in my past; not visiting art museums, halls of natural history and science, the mall in Washington DC, university collections; nothing, anywhere, ever, had prepared me for this. The Louvre, the Uffizi, the Met, the Rijksmuseum, the Victoria and Albert; all the great collections that I had ever visited shared common bonds of structure and organization. Their priceless artifacts were arranged in exhibits and encased in Plexiglas. There were guards patrolling the display areas, which were temperature and crowd controlled. Mostly, there was a cool and determined effort to create a mindset, to instruct the beholder in an appreciation of the materials exhibited. At the Cairo Museum, in 1980, piles of stuff lay everywhere, not guarded, not esteemed, and not cared for. The place was an oven. These were the treasures of ancient Egypt lying about, uncatalogued, dusty, and unprotected! Side rooms held piles of rubble. Tutankhamun's exhibit was the only one that was done up, because it had traveled to other countries. The wealth of treasures boggled the mind. The exhibit that had toured the U.S., grand as it had seemed, was paltry in comparison to the totality found in Cairo. Sarcophagus upon sarcophagus, in solid gleaming gold, their weight measuring in tons. There were chariots and jewelry and realistic funerary paintings and masks. At the Vatican, the glass-encased mummies of the popes had looked like the bones of little people turning to dust. These sarcophagus paintings were rich with color and light and expression, the paintings so detailed and vivid that it was like gazing on the real face. Perhaps this was the origin of the custom of rooms for overnight guests in the tombs. Going to view the sarcophagus of a departed loved one was like seeing the beloved animated by life again. Touching, heart-rending, and inspiring.

Outside the sun was shining. We walked the streets of Cairo, my American husband and I. Smiling Egyptian after Egyptian came up to my husband to shake his American hand. Cabbies beeped their horns and gaily waved their handkerchiefs. Citizens approvingly beamed in our direction. Everywhere horns honked and people gestured. "Hey, Americans," they would yell, smiling and waving. Our president had mediated a miracle, Egypt and Israel would be forever remembered in history as the countries that bridged the gap of hatred between Muslim and Jew. The era of détente had arrived.

At long last, peace had come to the Middle East.

# ABOUT THE AUTHOR

Sixty-two countries on six continents and counting. Every state in the union but two. Jeanne D'Brant began her travels in the back seat of her parents' car and was flying solo by the age of seventeen. She was captivated by Afghanistan between its wars, undertaking an epic ten-thousand-mile journey on public transportation across the burning deserts of the Middle East and the Khyber Pass. She flew the length of the Sahara four times, eagle eyes tracking camel caravans across the sands. Her three years in the sky as the airline industry was transitioning from the glory days of stewardessing to cattle car charters earned her eighty trips to Europe and a chance to transport the Muslim faithful on Hajj to Mecca. Out over the Tenezrouft with engine trouble, stormed upon landing by stranded Hajjis intent on hijack, she has witnessed scenes that few others can readily imagine. A journey into China brought home her beloved daughter and completed a family legend. Jeanne was charmed by the fumaroles, ferns, and kangaroos of Oceania on route to her Australian son's wedding. Off the coast of Tahiti in 2016, battling currents sweeping her flimsy boat to Antarctica, she made a vow that her future travels would be far more circumspect if she escaped the watery abyss. She loves low altitude propellor flights over mountain ranges, including the Kootenays of British Columbia and South Africa's Drakensberg. Before Covid, Jeanne led biology field-immersion tours to the rain forests of Central and South America and the Galapagos.

Dr. D'Brant is a chiropractor and board-certified clinical nutritionist who was voted Long Island's Alternative Doctor of the Year. She has studied Ayurveda in India and Traditional Chinese Medicine in China. Biochemistry, the dance of molecules, is her passion. She has been published in the fields of nutrition and autism, phytopharmacology, and other genres; her license renewal courses for health professionals were published internationally. Jeanne is an anatomy and biology professor, a published poet, nonfiction writer, and a former dance performer.

# SELECTED BIBLIOGRAPHY

1- **Orkin, Ruth.** "An American Girl in Italy." Iconic photo, Florence, 1951.

2- **Herbert, Frank.** Dune. Philadelphia, Chilton Books, 1965.

3- **Folktale Collection.** "The Arabian Nights." India and Persia, 8th century

4- **Frost, Robert.** "The Road Not Taken." Edward Connery, Lathem, 1916

5- **Dante, Alighieri, Musa, Mark.** Dante's Inferno. Bloomington, Indiana University Press, 1971.

6- **Dante, Alighieri, Musa, Mark.** Dante's Inferno.

7- **Whitman, Walt.** "Song of the Open Road." Leaves of Grass, 1856.

8- **Prine, John.** "John Prine," album, Atlantic Records, 1971.

9- **Mandela, Winnie, Benjamin, Anne, Benson, Mary.** Part of my Soul Went with Him. W.W. Norton, 1984.

10- **Shakespeare, William.** William IV, Part 2, Act 2

11- **Brodie, Fawn.** The Devil Drives: A Life of Sir Richard Burton. New York, Norton, 1967.

12- **Mundy, Talbot.** King of the Khyber Rifles. Bobbs-Merrill, 1916.

13- **LucasFilm.** Star Wars, Episode IV, 1977.

14- **Guru Nanak** Dev Ji. Doctrine of Sikhism, 15ᵗʰ Century, p. 473.

15- **Seeger,** Bob. "Beautiful Loser," album, 1975.

16- **James,** William. The Varieties of Religious Experience: A Study in Human Nature. Gifford Lectures, Edinburgh, 1901-02.

17- **Hendrix,** Jimmy. "Purple Haze," single by the Jimi Hendrix Experience, 1967.

18- **Ibsen,** Henrik. "Selected Poems." Translated by Northam, 1902.

19- **Preston,** Billy, **Fisher,** Bruce. "You are so Beautiful to Me," The Kids and Me album, 1974.